T0068168

Health and Wealth: God's Will or Not?

Health and Wealth: God's Will or Not?

Woody Stieffel

HEALTH AND WEALTH: GOD'S WILL OR NOT?

iUniverse books may be ordered through booksellers or by contacting:

iUniverse
1663 Liberty Drive
Bloomington, IN 47403
www.iuniverse.com
844-349-9409

Bible verses used are taken from King James Version (KJV) and New American Std. Bible (NASB).

ISBN: 978-1-6632-5936-3 (sc)
ISBN: 978-1-6632-5935-6 (e)

Library of Congress Control Number: 2023924600

Print information available on the last page.

iUniverse rev. date: 01/10/2024

Contents

Contents

Introduction

I am a 69 year old born again Christian who has been active in a variety of churches for 47 years. I have been a pastor of three churches for a total of 11 of those years. I have a 4 year BS degree in civil engineering from University of Mississippi. I also have 2 years of post graduate education from Moody Bible Institute and Hyles Anderson College. Observing Christians in America during that time has given me cause to worry about our collective spiritual state. One disturbing trend is the lack of knowledge of Bible truth. I am concerned that we as a people will perish for lack of that knowledge. It seems that only a small minority of church-going Americans have read the Bible through even once. This makes us vulnerable to every wind of doctrine that blows across our land. I am not an expert sociologist and certainly not an expert on the Bible. But I do enjoy trying to present the Bible in a simple and enjoyable way. It has always been enjoyable to me, even after having read it through 27 times to date. Bible preaching and teaching has been a part of my life for over 30 years.

I am the second of ten children. Our father is Ray Stieffel, Jr., who has also published his book, The Fantastic Muse and Other Stories, through iUniverse. I have admired his writing since I was a child and have always wanted to be a writer like him. This desire finally connected with my spiritual concerns and resulted in Health and Wealth: God's Will or Not?

I am a widower and live in Bay St. Louis, Mississippi. I enjoy the water and love sailing.

Currently attending First Baptist Church in Bay St. Louis. I worked a dual career for a number of years as an engineer and a pastor. Still working full time. The only problem is trying to figure out how to design a business card for that.

"When he saw the multitudes, he was moved with compassion on them."

Mark 9:36

Health and Wealth: God's Will or Not?

Of course it is. Like any good Father, God wants His children to be healthy and have everything they need. We know from the Bible that God *"does not afflict willingly, nor grieve the children of men"*, and that *"God is not willing that any should perish"*. God is not pleased to see any of his frail creatures suffer. Remember, Jesus answered the leper's plea, *"I will; be thou clean."* Surely it is not God's will that any should have cancer, diabetes, arthritis or be destitute, broke or struggling financially. If this is so, a lot of us must be out of God's will.

God *"rejoices with them that do rejoice and weeps with them that weep"*. It would seem that God above anyone else *"remembers them that suffer adversity as being (Himself) also in the body"*. When we hurt, God hurts with us. *"Jesus wept."* We most certainly do have a high priest who is *"touched with the feeling of our infirmities"*. Now here's a quality we'd do well to imitate and cultivate, as when the good Samaritan saw the wounded man, and *"he had compassion on him"*.

We can see a lot of empathy and compassion in the life of Jesus, who is *"the express image"* of the Father. Crowds of mostly poor and ailing folk followed Jesus around Galilee. In Matthew 9:36, it is reported that *"when he saw the multitudes, he was moved with compassion on them, because they fainted, and were scattered abroad, as sheep having no shepherd"*. Some get the notion that all God's interested in is our spiritual condition. However, it seems clear from this passage that he also pitied them for their physical suffering: "*because they fainted.*"

On another occasion, as Jesus was entering the city of Nain, He encountered a funeral procession. On seeing the heart-broken mother of the deceased man, we read that Jesus "*had compassion on her, and said unto her, 'Weep not'.*" (Luke 7:13) You may recall that Jesus raised the dead man back to life. (If we cannot raise a dead body back to life, we can still have compassion on the bereaved.) Here is compassion, not just for the hurting masses of humanity, but for one grieving mom. Here is compassion and tenderness, not just for those who dutifully "*seek first the kingdom of God and his righteousness*", but for a woman of whom we're told neither good nor bad. In other words, Jesus' compassion is arbitrary and universal just as the Father, who "*makes his sun to rise on the evil and the good and sends rain on the just and on the unjust*". (Matthew 5:45) Lucky for us.

In Jesus' parable of the ungrateful debtor who owed 10,000 talents (Matthew 18:23-35), He relates how the king was "*moved with compassion*" toward the servant and forgave him that vast debt. Here, Jesus' compassion is brought one step further. Not only does he have compassion on worthy folks (as the centurion) and even arbitrarily on people in general, but here he has compassion on the expressly *un*-deserving. That is, he willingly relieves a person's troubles even when the mess they're in is their own fault. It was the same compassion that said, "*Father, forgive them*". Likewise it is the compassion and "*goodness of God that leads us to repentance*". God is kind, good and compassionate to us all, deserving or not. This is really great news!

Merciful qualities like compassion and empathy are not to be only toward the innocent, as when Pharaoh's daughter opened Moses' basket and "*behold the babe wept. And she had compassion on him.*" The exercising of Christian virtues ought to depend entirely upon the character of the giver, not on the object of kindness. God loves because God *is* love, not because we're so lovable or because we need His love. God demonstrates compassion toward us because He *is* compassionate. Even before God created man, He was love and compassion just waiting to happen.

So we may infer from the very character of God that it is not His will that man suffer. In fact, we may deduce from the first pages of the Bible that God, so far letting man suffer, seemed to plan for his exquisite pleasure. First, God created man with an incredible capacity for pleasure and joy. Consider also that God evidently planned for man's happiness by placing him in such a paradise as Eden, where lived *"every tree that is pleasant to the sight and good for food"*. Then when God saw that it was not good for the man to be alone, He said, *"I will make him a help (fit) for him"*. God supplied Adam's every need.

We may turn to the other end of the Bible and similarly conclude: even after man's fall, God sought to remedy our well-deserved malady. I Peter 2:24 explains that Christ *"bore our sins in his own body on the tree... by whose stripes you were healed"*.

Not only does Christ have perfect compassion, but he can have perfect empathy. That is, he can perfectly relate to our hurts. He suffered in similar ways as we do, *"was in all points tempted like as we are"*. (Hebrews 4:15) Not only did he endure like trials and sufferings, but on the cross he received our precise, individual sins in his body, *"bore our sins in his own body"*.

Thus the Lamb of God who would take away the sin of the world shared our exact sins, bore the corresponding guilt and shame and even experienced the horror of utter alienation from his Father, *"My God, my God, why have you forsaken me?"*

So Jesus hurts when we hurt, grieves when we grieve, has a tooth-ache when we have a tooth-ache. This is the perfect *"friend that sticks closer than a brother"*. (Proverbs 18:24)

> *"The Great Physician now is near, the sympathizing Jesus;*
> *He speaks the drooping heart to cheer,*
> *Oh hear the voice of Jesus.*
> *Sweetest note in seraph song, sweetest name on mortal tongue;*
> *Sweetest carol ever sung, Jesus, blessed Jesus."*

Back to the original question: is it God's will that we be healthy and wealthy? So far all the evidence says yes. Even after Adam and Eve botched things up, our compassionate heavenly Father made provision for our salvation and happiness. Again and again, God repairs the ruin man makes of his life – to this day. In his kindness He clothed Adam and Eve with the skins. In His grace He clothes us with the very goodness of Christ. In His mercy He said in Noah's day, *"I will not again curse the ground any more for man's sake"*. (Genesis 8:21) Later in the fullness of time He sent His son into the world to save us from our sins.

> *"He comes to make his blessings flow far as the curse is found"*.

So in the long view of things, there is ample evidence that God *does* seek the well-being and happiness of man. *"You will show me the path of life: in your presence is fullness of joy; at your right hand there are pleasures forevermore."* (Psalm 16:11) His pleasant thoughts toward us are as numerous as the sands of the sea. Without dispute, God's will for us is *"joy unspeakable and full of glory"*. *"For I know the thoughts I think toward you, says the Lord, thoughts of peace and not of evil"*. (Jeremiah 29:11)

"No man can serve two masters…
you cannot serve God and (money)."

Jesus

Defining The Issue

America is unique in history. We are by far the wealthiest, most prosperous people in the history of the human race. Collectively, twenty-first century United States (so far) has the most robust economy.[2] According to Wikipedia, in 2022, the US owned 31% of the world's wealth, while having 4% of the world's population.[3]

In Solomon's day, Jerusalem was extremely wealthy so that *"the king made silver to be in Jerusalem as stones"* for abundance. But the standard of living would not compare to the U.S. today. Personally, I'd trade all that silver for one good air-conditioner.

We got where we are by the grace of God and, to America's credit, by hard work. In Solomon's case, the wealth was from the spoils of war. In the healthy economic climate we enjoy today, some problems come with the good. We seem to have degenerated spiritually as much as we have prospered materially. For example, our grandparents chose to become teachers, doctors and ministers for the virtue in the profession. Today's graduates are becoming lawyers, business professionals and investment strategists for the money in the profession. Whatever happened to men finding a sense of self-worth based on their contribution *to* society, rather than on acquisitions *from* society? Whatever happened to women finding their identity in raising their children well, rather than in developing a professional identity of their own? The best measure of a man is not how much he gets, but how much he gives. It's more honorable to *help* much than to *have* much.

We have degenerated spiritually. There is something incongruous about the Christian artist who composes a piece of worship music which they say God gave to them, while the copyright states, "*All rights reserved. Absolutely no reproduction allowed. Violators will be prosecuted to the maximum extent of the law.*" Better play it safe and not hum the tune in public. Of all people, why couldn't a Christian (or his publisher) waive copyright protection and gladly let his work benefit as many people as possible? What have we become?

R. A. Torrey tells this story of Dwight L. Moody, the world renowned evangelist of the late 1800's. He had compiled and published a hymnal for use in his city-wide campaigns. So many hymnals sold that over $100,000 in royalties accrued. (That would be closer to a million dollars today.) Apparently, Moody had never enquired about the matter. Finally, the publishing company contacted him, asking what to do with his money. He replied that he didn't need it. Just keep it. No wonder God used D. L. Moody. What a contrast to some money-grubbing evangelists of today.

I. Evidence of Materialism.

Everywhere we look there are symptoms of increasing appetite for making it big in life and making it fast. Nearly 40% of American households now invest in the stock market. Parents now work at two, three and more sources of income not just to feed the family, but to feed the investments. We seem to have degenerated into a financial feeding frenzy.

Our obsession for wealth is evidenced by the inordinate popularity of such T.V. shows as "Who Wants to Be a Millionaire?" and "Joe Millionaire". Watching such shows tends to fuel our greed.

Though it is very bad math to patronize casinos and lotteries, still the 1990's saw this turn into multi-billion dollar "industry". In 1996, more money was spent in the U. S. on gambling than on attending all sports events, going to movies, going to theme parks, playing video games and purchasing recorded music *combined!*[3] Gambling is commonly a case of the poor giving to the rich and supposedly enjoying it.

Book stores are burgeoning with hundreds of new books on how to get rich. How do you like some of these titles: It's About the Money, Get Your Share or Get a Financial Life? Now doesn't that inspire you to noble principle?

Or how about: Don't Die Broke, The Rich Die Richer and You Can Too or Smart Women Finish Rich? If the contents are as amusing as the titles, I might get a copy. Here's one I like: An Idiot's Guide to Making Millions on the Internet. At least this title is honest.

The problem is: America is a fertile market for such books. We've become so money-minded and investment oriented, it's a wonder how we sleep at all at night. Come to think of it, I think I'll buy stock in Sominex.

Americans voraciously seek both the substance and the symbols of wealth. Some feel sub-standard if they're not living in a fine upscale home and driving a late model car. People get so vain, it's almost comical. If we can't *be* rich, we want folks to *think* we are. We're surrounded by aristocrat wannabes. What a tiresome job to be busied with. Jesus prescribes, "*Come unto me all you that labor* (to keep your image thus inflated) *and are heavy laden…and learn of me; for I am meek and lowly in heart: and you shall find rest unto your souls*". (Matthew 11:28, 29) What a wearisome task it is, constantly trying to inflate the leaky balloon of our ego.

For many who feel like they are a nobody, life consists of trying to make everybody *think* they are a somebody. But "*in Christ*", everybody already is a somebody, though each should make themselves out to be a nobody. You know, the kind of nobody who would wash the feet of his friends, or would take on the role of a servant. Let's beware lest our society turn into a modern "Vanity Fair".

It's time for some of us to start thinking outsides the lines. There's more to life than pursuing the so-called American dream of becoming rich. The unspoken objective seems to be: whoever has the most money at the end wins. This kind of thinking almost guarantees us an unhappy dead-end. Choosing more worthy goals will surely result in a happier, fuller life. "*A good name is rather to be chosen than great riches, and loving favor rather than silver and gold.*" (Proverbs 22:1) Why not give up the lesser treasure: "*great riches*" and "*silver and gold*" to obtain the greater: "*a good name*" and "*loving favor*"? A good reputation and a wide circle of friends would certainly be more worthy goals and more gratifying.

Sadly, the materialistic mindset has found its way into America's churches. Too many church meetings today are little more than a financial seminar with a get rich scheme. Although Jesus said "*You cannot serve God and money*", many try.

Christians are in this world, but too many *love* this world. Christians who *do* love this world and the things that are in the world may be identified by

A. Their exempting themselves from giving financially to their church because they give their services to the church. But helping type up the bulletin or mowing the grass is not giving the first fruits of our increase. In many cases, the real problem is that they would rather give *anything* but money. Yet consider the impoverished apostles: they gave themselves entirely to the ministry, yet also gave out of their meager funds. (John 13:29)
B. Their excusing themselves from financial giving because they have so little. Yet the churches of Macedonia gave out of "*their deep poverty*" and "*abounded unto the riches of their liberality,*

> *For to their power ... and beyond their power they were willing of themselves ... but first gave their own selves to the Lord.*" (II Corinthians 8:2-5) Once they gave themselves to the Lord, they had no problem giving everything else. If we have so little as one talent, we are still to trade (invest) it. And what better place to invest than in the gospel? Let the poor give their widow's mite and those of ability give their ointment of spikenard.

America's obsession with possession makes us fertile ground for the doctrine of health and wealth. Our appetite for affluence makes us predisposed to accept it. We "buy" into the concept more for its appeal, than for its accuracy. I imagine very few really check it out in the Scriptures as the Boreans who "*were more noble than those in Thessalonica in that they received the word with all readiness of mind and searched the Scriptures daily* (to see) *whether those things were so*". (Acts 17:11)

Whatever the intentions of its preachers, it is important to consider ...

II. The Effect of Health and Wealth Preaching.

Even if the proponents of this doctrine mean well and intend the prosperity of others, the effect can be disastrous. First, to preach and insinuate that God wants all his children to be financially wealthy breeds materialism in Christians, which is the *last* thing that needs encouraging in an American. Materialism is the kudzu of the soul. So far from needing any cultivating, it needs to be beaten back daily so it won't take us over.

Secondly, it gives the wrong impression that one goal of Christianity is to prosper financially; whereas Jesus said that upon our consideration of following him, we should note that the Son of man had no where to lay his head. Rather, to follow Jesus and to be in step with him, we must deny ourselves and take up our cross.

In contrast, the effect of scriptural preaching on this subject would be to:

a. foster a detachment from the things of this world,
b. promote a guarded wariness against the love of money and abundance,
c. encourage compassion toward the poor,
d. properly set one's affection on heavenly things,
e. comfort the minds of many who struggle financially.

Ministers are called upon to declare all the counsel of God. They are to address such a wide range of subjects as: how to obtain eternal life, the second coming of Christ, dealing with depression, raising children, handling persecution, confronting sin, marriage relationships, personal ethics, work principles, etc. Some preachers, however, seem to get locked in on one subject. No matter how the message may start off, it always seems to gravitate back to that one subject. Health and wealth preachers fall into this rut as much as any other. Too many of them preach on little else than money and prosperity. Testimonies and illustrations are almost exclusively about how God supposedly has given them money or increase of material goods. So little do we hear out of their mouths a testimony of someone receiving Christ or of someone turning from their sin. But out of the abundance of the heart must the mouth speak. Money is on their mind, so wealth is in their words.

In Psalm 45:1, the heart of the *"ready writer"* was *"inditing a good matter"*. The Hebrew word, *rachash,* translated *"inditing"*, indicates that he was bubbling over with a thought. His heart is overflowing with a vision of one *"fairer than the children of men"* whom *"God has blessed... forever"* and *"has anointed...with the oil of gladness above (his) fellows"*. It is a vision of his Messiah and our Savior. This should be the abundance of our heart, our delight and *"exceeding great joy"*. Sadly, some preachers are not so full of love for the excellent Jesus as the faithful psalmist was. Let's see to it that our hearts are full of him.

We too easily become like Demas, of whom Paul said, *"Demas has forsaken me, having loved this present world."* (II Timothy 4:10) Remember when Nebuchadnezzar walked in the palace and said, *"Is not this great Babylon that I have built for the house of my kingdom by the might of my power and for the honor of my majesty?"* (Daniel 4:30) How many pastors and corporation C.E.O.s have similarly appraised the work of their hands? Our heart easily swells with pride at our accomplishments, rather than credit God who gives the increase.

Our tendency to gloat over successes must put God in a real fix. He loves us with such kindness and tenderness, and loves to give us prosperity and abundance. He is pleased to see His children prosperous and happy. Yet in some cases, when He so blesses us, we turn idolatrously and adulterously away from Him, and come to love the gift more than the Giver.

III. Have We Become Laodicea?

Some students of prophecy take the seven churches of Revelation 2 & 3 to correspond to distinct ages of the church. The church in the city of Laodicea, being the last of them would correspond to the last age of the church, which many believe to be the times we now live in. Jesus taught us to observe the signs of our times so that we may be aware of his imminent return. In Revelation 3:15-19, we may observe what are the traits of the end time church:

a. It is a lukewarm church. (v. 16.) That is, the end time church is neither on fire for God, nor cold and distant from God. They stay just warm or close enough to God to appease their conscience. They attend church, go through the motions, but are quite lackluster in their affection and devotion.

b. They are a wealthy church.
c. They have a good opinion of themselves.
d. Spiritually, they are in bad shape.

I say America's churches can plead guilty on all four counts. What is it going to take to bring us back to humility, to our first love, to our first works? What will it take to cure us of our obsessive materialism? Does God need to raise up Elijah to pray for no rain? Will God have to break us with another Great Depression? Or will God have to raise up adversaries against us as He raised up Hadad and Jeroboam to be adversaries against Solomon?

Throughout the history of the kings of Israel, beginning with Solomon, we can see there is no test like prosperity. It worked idolatry in Solomon, collapse to Rehoboam, vanity to Uzziah, carelessness in Hezekiah and eventually the utter collapse of the nation Israel. As prosperity continues in America, let us who are the salt beware that it no longer breeds materialism, immorality, corruption, and spiritual lethargy. Such will inevitably lead to the demise and collapse of this nation as well. Can we stem the tide of infectious greed, love of money, self-serving and merciless business practice? Our survival may very well depend on it.

Well, there's a spiritual perspective of the state of the union. It is in such a climate that the doctrine arises that God wants us to be healthy and wealthy.

America, America, may God thy gold refine,
Till all success be nobleness, and every gain divine.

"And he gave them their request; but sent leanness into their soul."

(Psalm 106:15)

Does God Want Me to have the Best?

The idea that "God wants me to have the best" is being preached throughout our land, though largely unchallenged. I have the feeling that not too many people give a second thought to this "health and wealth" concept. It sounds nice enough like it is. If there were any message which ears would be itching to hear, this would be it. Why would somebody want to check the scriptural accuracy of something they already like? It's time *"that we henceforth be no more children, tossed to and fro, and carried about with every wind of doctrine, by the sleight of men, and cunning craftiness, whereby they lie in wait to deceive."* (Ephesians 4:14)

Well, does God want me to have the best? More to the point is whether *I* want me to have the best and whether God would let me. Too often, the case is that we have such a lust in our eyes for the so called "finest" things of life and want to believe that God also wants us, or at least allows us, to have them. (We say "finest" to dignify our greed.) It is usually out of a covetous heart that we ask amiss and *"consume it upon our lusts"*. There are times when God gives us our request, but sends leanness into our soul. Commonly, the leanness is contracted from what was requested.

For example, consider the prodigal (wasteful) son of Luke 15. The first words out of his mouth are, *"Father, give me"*. Here's a man who would fit in well with twenty-first century America. He wants instant gratification, wealth before work, promotion before performance. Later, when he comes to his senses, the first words out of his mouth are, *"Father, I have sinned"*. In the between times, he certainly had *"leanness of soul."* He also had leanness of body, *"I perish with hunger"*.

Next, consider that America was probably never healthier spiritually than in the pioneer days of the mid 1700's. Those were the days of the Great Awakening. Our forefathers were by no means wealthy and hardly comfortable in standard of living. Yet they matured spiritually as Israel in the wilderness. Hardships made them of sturdy constitution both physically and spiritually.

Today though, God has granted our request for bodily comforts, security and ease, and we've come to leanness of soul. Evidence of this? If the spiritual pulse of America may be measured by the caliber of prime time TV, we're sure enough in bad shape. These days, a scarlet letter "A" would be a badge of honor instead of disgrace. Adultery and fornication, rather than being condemned, is being condoned. In our early days, national leaders *"more than self their country loved and mercy more than life"*. No wonder God shed His grace on America. Today our nation is torn by partisan and personal interests. Pork barrel politics degrade our nation's best interests into regional favoritism. America's morality has so eroded that we'd rather be rich than right. Now we live as if rich *is* right.

Even the soul of America's churches has grown sadly lean. Too many have more appetite for entertainment than for edification. God has given us our request so that we are *"rich and increased with goods and have need of nothing"*. Yet we are stricken with leanness of soul and are *"wretched and miserable and poor and blind and naked"*. (Revelation 3:17)

We are fast becoming the prodigal sons of our forefathers – wasteful and extravagant. We either waste our *"substance with riotous living"* or we squander it on *"purple and fine linen and fare sumptuously every day"*. Consider the effect of this indulgent living. Just as we get sleepy after a big dinner, so when we have gratified ourselves with every conceivable delight, we slip into a spiritual snooze. We become dull of hearing. We are unaware of our spiritual decline, like Samson who *"knew not that the Lord was departed from him."* (Judges 16:20)

Sure God wants us to enjoy life, but too much of a good thing is not good. Too much of this life's sensual pleasures is not good for us. We should be moderate in all things.

We're in bad enough shape just having an appetite for the worldly pleasures around us. Such a sweet tooth will get us in trouble. Bible commentator Matthew Henry puts it this way, "But if your heart be set upon the earth and the things of it, it is to be feared that you have your treasure and portion in it."[3] (Matthew Henry Commentary, Vol. V, p. 714) That would be saying you have no portion or place in heaven.

We are exhorted to set our *"affection on things above, not on things on the earth"*. (Colossians 3:2) Just what you wanted to hear today: if you're enjoying life, you're in big trouble. Well not exactly. The point is more like: no candy before supper. Why do we tell our kids that? Because too much sweets before supper will ruin their appetite for better things. *"It is not good to eat much honey."* (Proverbs 25:27)

God most certainly does want us to have the best – but not yet, or maybe, not here. When Gehazi lied to Namaan to get free money and clothes, Elisha reproved him with these words, *"Is it a time to receive money, and to receive garments, and oliveyards, and vineyards, and sheep, and oxen, and men servants, and maid servants?"* (II Kings 5:26) (This is probably exactly what Gehazi was dreaming of at the moment.) How much more should we be detached from this world, having more sure promises from Christ of better things to come! Of all people, Christians in these end times ought to say,

> *"This world is not my home; I'm just a passing through.*
> *My treasures are laid up somewhere beyond the blue."*

Does God want me to have the best? Yes, but His best is not a late model Lexus or a half million dollar home. His best would be those treasures laid up in heaven. Why not give up what we cannot keep to gain what we cannot lose?

Someone may ask the question this way: "Does God want *me* to have the best? Somebody's got to have it; why not me?" The reasoning goes something like this: "Obviously, God wants me to have plenty, because I've *been* getting plenty. All this blessing and in-gathering is clear evidence of divine favor." "God wants *me* to have the best or plenty because I *do* have it." Believe me, many think this way. But the logic is faulty for three reasons:

A. **Present prosperity is not necessarily an indication of God's favor.** Neither does lack of it show His dis-favor. For He sends his rain on the just and on the unjust. Solomon also observed *"there be just men, unto whom it happens according to the work of the wicked: again, there be wicked men, to whom it happens according to the work of the righteous."* (Ecclesiastes 8:14) There are crooked and honest folks among both rich and poor. Jesus sometimes gives a tasty sop to someone about to betray him.
B. **It is a mistaken notion that whatever happens is God's will.** The fact that an event *does* happen does not mean God *wanted* it to happen. *"It is not the will of your Father in heaven, that one of these little ones should perish."* (Matthew 18:14) Yet people

perish every day. No sin ever committed is God's will, yet we do it every day. In so many ways, our lives do not develop along the ideal paths God had planned. But in His infinite wisdom, He is able to cause all things to work together for good, even when we may have intended evil, as when Joseph's brothers sold him and God turned it out for good. God may have allowed us to get considerable wealth, but it does not reasonably follow that He intended for us to keep it all.

C. **God does not necessarily show His favor by increasing our goods of this world.** God showed His favor to Paul by giving visions of the third heaven; to Peter and John, power to heal; to generous Barnabas, success in ministry. Now shall we look for our reward to be monetary? This would be giving us a stone instead of bread. Maybe even a stumbling stone. When we think of how much temptation and snares come with wealth, it would seem more like a sign of Satan's favor. Material acquisitions so often pierce us through with many sorrows, as in the case of the prodigal son. Remember also that the abundance of gold which Rehoboam inherited from Solomon became occasion for the sacking of Jerusalem. Some blessing.

Does God want me to have the best? Yes, but by *His* definition of the word. Wealth and lands and goods are not God's best because they do not satisfy very much or very long. *"He that loves silver shall not be satisfied with silver; nor he that loves abundance with increase: this is also vanity."* (Ecclesiastes 5:10) Yet what God gives *does* satisfy, so that we do not thirst again. (See John 4:14.) Surely Jesus would rather give us those good and perfect gifts which come from above. His best gifts would be those that do the best *for* us. Wealth tends to make us more haughty than holy. Have you met anyone like that?

In Revelation 3:17 and 18, we find a distinction between what man thinks is best and what God says is best. *"Because you say, I am rich, and increased with goods, and have need of nothing; and know not that you are wretched, and miserable, and poor, and blind, and naked: I counsel you to buy of me gold tried in the fire, that you may be rich; and white raiment, that you may be clothed, and that the shame of your nakedness do not appear; and anoint your eyes with eyesalve, that you may see."*

These verses are part of the letter to Laodicea. This church is wealthy materially, but impoverished spiritually. Notice the first thing this church says, *"I am rich."* Rich folks want everybody to know it. It is said first because it is foremost in their mind. They are rich, proud of it, and proud to proclaim it. It is sad that of all people, the church should have such poorly placed values. Yet how many times have we been asked, "How is your church doing?" And we reply, "Great, our offerings are up."

However, God's assessment of them is very different, *"You are wretched...and poor"*. How did they get to be in such bad shape? Probably by neglecting God in their pursuit of wealth. He says they are poor because His eye is more on their heavenly holdings, while their mind is fixated on their earthly gains. It is for this short-sightedness that Jesus says they are ignorant, *"you...know not."* If we could but know these things!

In verse 18, Jesus counsels them to seek after better things, or rather, these best things. What was best in man's eyes left him *"wretched... miserable... poor...blind... and naked."* Notice, in contrast, that God's best leaves man truly rich, clothed and unashamed, anointed and having spiritual vision. All these are lasting, enduring benefits for the believer.

Yes, God wants you to have the best. However, God's best is not external, transitory goods. Rather, His best for you is more like compassion, wisdom, well-developed love, spiritual gifts, potent prayer and eternal life.

"For your sakes he became poor, that you through his poverty might be made rich."

II Corinthians 8:9

How Rich was Jesus?

One of the foremost arguments presented by proponents of "Health and Wealth" is the contention that Jesus was rich. Some say Jesus was so rich, that he kept his money in a treasury. They say that he wore the equivalent of designer clothing, referring to the seamless tunic he wore. This chapter explores those claims Biblically. Two issues surface in addressing this question. First, how rich was Jesus? Second, how would his living wealthy justify our doing the same? Stay tuned for the exciting conclusion. It will be good news.

Let's start with Jesus' origin. Some folks do not realize that Jesus Christ did not begin his existence at his birth or conception. According to the Bible, he existed long before even the creation of heaven and earth. His *"goings forth have been from of old, from everlasting"*. (Micah 5:2) Jesus put it this way, *"Before Abraham was, I am."* (John 8:58) Later he prayed, *"And now, O Father, glorify thou me with your own self with the glory which I had with thee before the world was"*. (John 17:5) Translation: "Father, now restore the glory we shared before the world was made."

I. Jesus Was Rich In Spirit

This is an important point and it is beyond dispute that Jesus was "rich" beyond human imagination from eternity past. He owned all those *"riches in glory"*. *"True riches"*, not *"uncertain riches"*; imperishable treasure in heaven, not perishable material treasure which moth and rust do corrupt; sure possessions, which thieves may not break through to steal.

What were these riches which Jesus enjoyed for ages past? First, a perfect love relationship with his Father. In both visage and spirit, He is *"altogether lovely."* There is always a perfect and deep understanding of each other, the lack of which is a great frustration among human relationships. There is at all times a perfect coinciding of desires, values, knowledge and even works. *"I do always those things that please Him." "I and my Father are one."* (John 8:29 and 10:30) Like the perfectly synchronized gyrations of figure skaters, Jesus and the Father act together, think together and love together. Part of what made Calvary a misery was the suspension of this perfect love relationship. Their perfect *love* could not be broken, but the fellowship was momentarily broken. This was in order to restore the broken relationship between us and the Father. *"The just (died) for the unjust that he might bring us to God."* (I Peter 3:18)

Second, Jesus shared a wondrous *"glory which (he) had with (the Father) before the world was"*. This adds the element of mutual awe to their relationship. They share the joy of wonder, admiration and high majesty.

Remember that this was going on long before the world began, before material riches even existed. Now enter Jesus into the human race still trailing clouds of glory and retaining wisps of awareness of his heavenly origin. *"I must be about my Father's business."* He was as Moses returned from the mount except that he *"knew not that skin of his face shone as he talked with him"*. (Exodus 34:29) These two beheld the glory of the Father, though Moses saw only the *"back parts"*. Jesus had not only *"tasted of the heavenly gift...and the powers of the world to come"*, he owned it. How could the highest, finest of earthly delights hold any interest for the likes of Jesus and Moses? Matthew Henry puts it so admirably, *"Jesus was perfectly dead to the wealth of this world, the ease of the body, and the praise of men, and was wholly taken up with divine and heavenly things."* (Vol. V, p. 989) Let's aspire.

Anyone who has gotten a sure enough taste of fellowship with Jesus Christ should have such a disdain for the *"beggarly elements"* of this world. When Simon the sorcerer offered Peter some money, Peter not very tactfully replied, *"Thy money perish with thee!"* More ministers today need to have Peter's values. For Moses, Jesus and Peter, God was surely their *"exceeding great reward"* as He was for Abraham. These men are like children who are not allured at Christmas by the surrounding glitter, glamour and gifts of the season. Disinterested in their gifts, they embrace Mom and Dad proclaiming, "You're my treasure". You might be thinking, "In your dreams!" Well, why can't we be that way toward our heavenly Father? Having become a man, isn't it time we *"put away childish things?"* How much more worthy is He of our utmost gratitude and highest praise? God might sometimes give us much so as to test us, *"do you love me more than these?"*

Getting back to the question "How rich was Jesus?", we probably agree that he was rich beyond all measure, at least in the spiritual sense. But was he also rich in the material sense? Let's see what the record says. First, let's consider what prophecy foretold on this.

II. What Does Prophecy Say?

Deuteronomy 18:15 Far back in the ancient writings of Moses, he wrote of Jesus as he was moved by the Holy Ghost that God *"will raise up...a Prophet...like unto me."* Jesus' life and work did indeed come to resemble that of Moses:

1. It was said that Moses *"was a goodly child"*, while Jesus was a perfect child.

2. Pharaoh nearly killed Moses in slaying all the Hebrew baby boys and Herod sought to kill Jesus in killing all the infant boys around Bethlehem.
3. Moses grew up amid all the wealth of Pharaoh's house as the heir apparent, possibly the richest household in the old world. Jesus, as we discussed earlier, spent eternity past amid the glory and "wealth" of heaven.
4. Moses walked away from all the wealth, comfort and ease "*choosing rather to suffer affliction with the people of God, than to enjoy the pleasures of sin for a season; esteeming the reproach of Christ greater riches than the treasures in Egypt...by faith he forsook Egypt*". (Hebrews 11:25,27) In this very point Jesus was a prophet "*like unto Moses*". "*For your sakes he became poor, that you through his poverty might be made rich.*" (II Corinthians 8:9) Notice the verse says he *became* poor. This indicates that he was previously rich. When Jesus laid aside his glory and inhabited a body of flesh, he "*condescended to men of low estate*" in grace unsurpassed. Never before or since did anyone humble himself so greatly. Not even Emperor Nebuchadnezzar stooped so low (or rather was put so low) when he was deposed from the throne of Babylon to "*be with the beasts of the field*" seven years. Moses dwelt with sheep in the wilderness forty years. Jesus suffered the company of sinful men about 33 years. "*How long shall I suffer you?*" (Matthew 17:17)

Clearly, it is consistent with the prophecy of Deuteronomy 18:15 that Jesus was not materially wealthy in this life.

Next consider Joseph, maybe the most remarkable type (preview) of Christ in the Old Testament. Though he was one of the heirs of Jacob's vast wealth, he was brought very low and later highly exalted. He first made himself a servant of the lowest of men (in the prison), as Christ, who *"took upon himself the form of a servant"*. Though truly rich, Joseph lived in abject poverty. It was only after Joseph's "resurrection" from prison that God exalted him. Likewise with Jesus. It was after Jesus humbled himself that his Father *"divided him a portion with the great"*. Both men, upon their exaltation became a savior to many nations.

Isaiah 53 Consider the several facets of poverty and lowliness of Christ's life predicted here:

1. (v.2) ***"He has no form nor comeliness; and when we shall see him, there is no beauty that we should desire him."***
   The fact that Jesus had no physical appeal was a stumbling block to the Jews. Those who looked on the outward appearance rather than on the heart of Jesus did not desire him. Thus Jesus *"made himself of no reputation"*.
2. (v.3) ***"He is despised and rejected of men...and we esteemed him not."***
   Jesus did not bask in the limelight of popularity. If he had been a wealthy man, that alone would have made him many friends. *"Wealth makes many friends"* and *"many will entreat the favor of a prince."* It is no new thing that those who come wearing a *"gold ring"* and *"goodly apparel"* get more respect than the poor. Again it was Jesus' poverty and lack of airs that became a stumbling block for the Jews. Wealth and fine dress were closely equated with personal righteousness in Christ's time – and ours. When Jesus remarked, *"It is easier for a camel to go through the eye of a needle, than for a rich man to enter into the kingdom of God"*, the disciples were incredulous and exclaimed, *"Who then can be saved"*, (if not the righteous rich?)

3. (v. 12) ***"Therefore will I divide him a portion with the great, and he shall divide the spoil with the strong."***
   Notice the future tense of verses 11 and 12. The first ten verses of Isaiah 53, which detail Jesus' life and passion, are expressed in past tense, denoting his pre-resurrection state. The future tense of verses 11 and 12 correspond to his post resurrection state. Thus it is after he humbles himself that God highly exalts him. He shall divide the spoil after he secures the victory. But while the Captain of our salvation warred on our behalf, he did not *"entangle himself with the affairs of this life"*. Nor did he indulge himself with the pleasures of this world. Such would be unbefitting of military life. He demonstrated himself a sojourner in this world. Again in this verse, it seems that Jesus neither had, nor looked for, any *"portion"* in this life. Do your warfare and wage resemble his?

Generally, the tenor of all the prophecy of his first coming is the suffering servant, the oppressed and afflicted one, the lowly one who would come *"riding upon a colt, the foal of an ass"*. (Zechariah 9:9) All this is consistent with Jesus living his life in material poverty. Jesus, like Paul, came *"as poor, yet making many rich; as having nothing, and yet possessing all things"*. (II Corinthians 6:10) Consider the incongruity of a rich Jesus with these prophecies of a lowly Jesus. It just would not make sense.

Continuing our analysis of whether Jesus was materially rich, we now turn to the gospels, where we find some very definitive answers.

III. What do the Gospels Say?

Let's first consider the family Jesus was born into. Far from living as a well-to-do woman, Mary says *"Behold the handmaid of the Lord"* and marvels that God *"regarded the low estate of his handmaiden"*. (Luke

1:38,48) She was blessed in spirit and in destiny, but certainly not materially. Having little enough of her own affairs or possessions to attend to, she was at liberty to go wait on Aunt Elisabeth for three months. Behold also the handmaid of people. I wouldn't be surprised to find out that she even washed the feet of elderly Elisabeth, who probably would have had great difficulty doing so herself, being seven to nine months pregnant. Like his mother, Jesus also *"came not to be ministered unto but to minister"*. (Matthew 20:28)

Well how about Joseph? Did Mary marry into a wealthy family? Hardly. Joseph was a working class man, a carpenter by trade. Carpenters have never been known for their wealth. They usually build everybody else's empires.

Mary and Joseph also had four other sons and some unspecified number of daughters. *"And his sisters, are they not all with us?"* (Matthew 13:55,56) "All" would mean three or more sisters. So here's a carpenter raising at least eight children, just as likely ten or twelve. This does not sound like a recipe for getting rich.

Next, let's consider the circumstances of Jesus' birth. We note that Jesus was born in a stable. What an embarrassment! Now someone might object that Joseph had the money or he would not have applied for a room at the inn. True, but Providence had it that there were no rooms available at just the time Jesus was due. So even the idea of being displaced from home and having Jesus born in a motel room was not lowly enough to suit God. No, this gospel which was to be preached to the poor and received best by the poor, would, in its beginning, be very accommodating to the poor. The story of Jesus' birth would be told to the poorest, humblest people in the world and none would feel ashamed to embrace Christ as their savior because they had such humble origins. *"God so loved the world"* and in the lowly state of Jesus' birth, the gospel puts its arms around all the world.

Remember next that the announcement of Immanuel's arrival was not made to the mayor of Bethlehem or to the dignitaries of Jerusalem. Rather, word first came to shepherds – of all people. Smelly, poor shepherds. Maybe the angels figured shepherds would be better at finding mangers, while well-to-do folks might have disdained to visit a stable at all.

Some time later, though, an entourage of visitors from the east came to deliver gifts befitting a newborn king. They arrive at Joseph and Mary's house. I imagine they could not believe their eyes. "This can't be the right place. Let's check that sextant reading again." But they knew what the prophecies had said and they knew this was the right place. You see, they were wise men. Yet it was no new thing that the prince of God's people had such humble beginnings. Wasn't Moses found in a basket, Joseph promoted from prison and David called from the sheepcote? Gideon objected his unworthiness, *"Oh my Lord, wherewith shall I save Israel? Behold, my family is poor in Manasseh, and I am the least in my father's house."* (Judges 6:15)

Much more would all the princes of spiritual Israel (the church) be men lowly of mind and lowly of origin. Witness John the Baptist, *"the voice of one crying in the wilderness"*. Jesus later issued this edict of the kingdom, *"Whosoever will be great among you, let him be your minister; and whosoever will be chief among you, let him be your servant."* (Matthew 20: 26,27)

Well, was the holy family made rich with all that royal gold, frankincense and myrrh? There is no evidence that they began to have a life of comfort, ease or luxury. On the contrary, they immediately after fled for their lives into Egypt to escape Herod. I agree with those who figure the magi's gifts paid for the expenses of their flight into Egypt and sustained them there till they returned. Then it was back to Nazareth and to Joseph's old carpentry business.

There is virtually nothing written about Jesus' many years at Nazareth. God in His wisdom has left the veil to cover these silent years. We would likely have given an inordinate amount of attention to the childhood of Jesus.

Now let's analyze the record of the gospels and look for answers to the question:

IV. Did Jesus Become Rich In the Ministry?

In looking for clues about the lifestyle of Jesus as an adult, let's study sequentially through the four gospels and see if we can construct a clear picture. It is important to know how he lived, because we are not only to obey his commands, but to follow his example.

Beginning in the gospel of Matthew, Jesus first appears as an adult at his baptism. (Matthew 3:13-17) There is nothing in this passage to indicate whether he lived in plenty or poverty. We find this to be the case throughout a large part of the gospel record. There's a reason for this. Just as the Holy Spirit saw fit to reveal virtually nothing about the childhood of Jesus, so little is revealed to us about his personal life. Again, God wants our attention fixed on Christ, not fixated on his money, property or personal matters.

However, in this account of Jesus' baptism, we do see treasure beyond human comprehension bestowed on Jesus. "*The heavens were opened unto him*" and the Spirit of God descended upon him. It is this treasure God would have us desire. "*Covet earnestly the best gifts.*" It is this treasure God would give us. "*How much more shall your heavenly Father give the Holy Spirit to them that ask him.*" (Luke 11:13)

Matthew 4:1-11

1. *Then was Jesus led up by the Spirit into the wilderness to be tempted by the devil.*
2. *And when he had fasted forty days and forty nights, he was afterward hungry.*
3. *And when the tempter came to him, he said, If thou be the Son of God, command that these stones be made bread.*
4. *But he answered and said, It is written, Man shall not live by bread alone, but by every word that proceeds out of the mouth of God.*
5. *Then the devil takes him up into the holy city, and sets him on a pinnacle of the temple,*
6. *And says to him, If thou be the Son of God, cast yourself down; for it is written, He shall give his angels charge concerning you, and in their hands they shall bear you up, lest at any time you dash your foot against a stone.*
7. *Jesus said unto him, It is written again, You shall not tempt the Lord your God.*
8. *Again the devil takes him up into an exceedingly high mountain, and shows him all the kingdoms of the world, and the glory of them,*
9. *And says unto him, All these things will I give you, if you will fall down and worship me.*
10. *Then said Jesus unto him, Get thee hence, Satan, for it is written, You shall worship the Lord, your God, and him only shall you serve.*
11. *Then the devil leaves him, and, behold, angels came and ministered unto him.*

If Jesus ever lived wealthily or comfortably, it was anywhere but here. Led by the Spirit, Jesus makes himself destitute of every earthly comfort and convenience. Once he received the riches in glory at his baptism, he quite readily does without the comforts of this world in the wilderness. When fleshly appetites begin to rise in him, he says, *"Man shall not live by bread alone, but by every word that proceeds out of the mouth of God."* Thus he commends heavenly treasure above earthly necessities.

When Satan offers Jesus all the kingdoms of the world if he would worship him, it was the most spectacular offer ever made to a man. Many a man has forfeited his soul and many a man of God has compromised his ministry by accepting a similar offer. Today, Satan only asks a man to fall down and worship the wealth. Yet Jesus flatly refuses and runs him off. Balaam kept up dialogue with his tempters and eventually reconsidered. Jesus, who was willing to deny himself necessary food, was just as willing to deny himself unnecessary kingdoms and glory. The Son of man came not to be ministered unto.

It's interesting that Satan tempts Jesus to receive wrongly what God had promised to give him rightly. Satan offered to give Jesus all the kingdoms of the world. But in Psalm 2:8, the Father offers to the Son, *"Ask of me, and I shall give you the heathen (nations) for your inheritance and the uttermost parts of the earth for your possession."* Likewise, Satan tempts *us* to take wrongly or prematurely what God already plans to give us rightly and in the proper time.

Matthew 5:3 and 5

3. ***Blessed are the poor in spirit; for theirs is the kingdom of heaven.***
5. ***Blessed are the meek; for they shall inherit the earth.***

These words begin the great sermon on the mount. This marks the commencing of the preaching of the gospel to the poor, whom

Jesus addresses as *"poor in spirit"* and *"meek"*. Such qualities commonly characterize the poor. Much of Jesus' public life was spent in close contact with humble, poor folk. Or rather, the poor chose to be in contact with him. *"Has not God chosen the poor in this world to be rich in faith?"* (James 2:5) This being the case, it would be very strange for Jesus to live the plush, comfortable life of a rich man while constantly in the presence of the poor.

Matthew 6:19-21

19. ***Lay not up for yourselves treasures upon earth, where moth and rust do corrupt, and where thieves break through and steal,***

20. ***But lay up for yourselves treasures in heaven, where neither moth nor rust do corrupt, and where thieves do not break through nor steal;***

21. ***For where your treasure is, there will your heart be also.***

Our Lord gives the command and warning as clearly here as anywhere: *"lay not up for yourselves treasures upon earth."* Though he stated it so plainly, and its application is so obvious, yet he amplifies further with two very strong lines of reasoning.

First, treasure in this world is a poor investment. It is not secure, for *"thieves break through and steal"* and *"riches certainly make themselves wings (and) fly away as an eagle toward heaven."* (Proverbs 23:5) Our most miserly efforts to conserve or preserve our gains will avail nothing when God determines to scatter it: *"When you brought it home, I did blow upon it."* (Haggai 1:9) Treasure in this world also brings a poor return, for moth and rust diminish its value. Both we and our possessions *"do fade as a leaf."* (Isaiah 64:6) If we allow our treasure to stagnate or rust in this world, it shall be to our rebuke: *"Cast...the unprofitable servant into outer darkness."* We're better advised: *"Make to yourselves friends of the mammon (wealth) of unrighteousness; that when you fail, they may receive you into everlasting habitations."* (Luke 16:9)

Second, we ought to lay up treasure in heaven because then our heart will be in heaven - and later our soul. And later still, our body. *"Where your treasure is, there will your heart be."* If we forward our treasure to heaven, then we will have more of a heart for heaven, look more for heaven, labor more for heaven, and feel more sure of getting to heaven.

Conversely, if our treasure is on earth, then our heart will be also. Our mind will be on our money, our thoughts will be on our things, our eye will be on our earnings, slavishly so. Our heart will have little savor for the Savior, but have relish enough for the treasures and trifles of this world. In other words, we'll probably become as stagnant and corrupt as our rusted treasure.

So Jesus says, *"Lay not up for yourselves treasures upon earth."* It would seem very strange if Jesus were to teach us not to do such a thing and yet do so himself. This verse could nearly stand on its own in defeating the claim that Jesus was materially rich.

Matthew 8:1

When Jesus came down from the mountain, great multitudes followed him.

Nowhere do we read of Jesus renting or using coliseums or other fine or comfortable facilities. No, his church was the grassy mountain slopes and sandy sea shores. His pulpit was the prow of a boat or top of a boulder. He occasionally preached in the synagogues and in the temple, but these were more the exception than the rule. Usually his furnishings were humble and natural. Neither Jesus nor his ministry showed signs of wealth.

Matthew 8:20

And Jesus said unto him, the foxes have holes, and the birds of the air have nests; but the Son of man has not where to lay his head."

Jesus was replying to a scribe who had just expressed his desire to follow Jesus. However, Jesus would have him count the cost. He cautioned him that traveling about with an itinerant preacher would not be so comfortable and convenient a way of life to which he was probably accustomed. Jesus made it pretty clear that he had no certain dwelling place, not even so little as a tent, as the patriarchs. That would have been better than fox holes or bird nests.

Not only was following Christ not to be pursued as a means of gain, but his followers should count on not having the comforts others enjoy. Disciples of Christ are to endure these hardships as good soldiers. Nobody joins the Marines because it pays so well, but rather because they want to put themselves into valuable service.

Jesus may have had a normal home when he resided at Nazareth, but when he began to travel about preaching the gospel, the twelve apostles traveled with him as well as a number of women. At times hundreds and even thousands went with him, as we see in Matthew 8:1, "*Great multitudes followed him.*" There was no practical way for all of them to be housed each night as they visited the many cities, towns and villages of Israel. They likely just camped out each night, faring the best they could. It is inconceivable that the one who came not to be served, but to serve would have enjoyed the luxuries of his friends' hospitality, while his following slept just outside, exposed to the elements. Certainly, Jesus was as loyal to his comrades as Uriah who said, "*My lord Joab, and the servants of my lord, are encamped in the open fields; shall I then go into my house, to eat and drink, and to lie with my wife?*" (II Samuel 11:11) No, this Good Shepherd did abide in the field, keeping watch over his flock by night.

There are some in our time who maintain several homes for their private use: a summer home, a winter home, homes in different cities where they spend time. There are some who very wrongly attempt to ease their consciences and justify their excesses by claiming that Jesus owned several houses which he supposedly resided in when he preached in the area. Let me assure you that nothing in the scriptures even suggests such a thing. If Jesus had owned a house or had even stayed in others' houses, then the statement he made to this aspiring disciple would have been very misleading. Matthew 4:13 does state that when Jesus left Nazareth, *"he came and dwelt in Capernaum."* That's all it says. Scripture does not say whether he rented a house, owned a house, lived as a guest in a house or whether he lived in a house at all. It does seem from such verses as Matthew 9:10 and 28 that he did stay in a house when he was in Capernaum. At other times, he probably slept in the open as many shepherds did and as John the Baptist surely did.

In Matthew 13:1, it is mentioned that Jesus went *"out of the house and sat by the seaside."* Now this was in Capernaum, where Jesus resided. However, the expression cannot be taken as evidence that Jesus owned that house. It is possible that the house referred to was one he lived in. But more likely, he was simply visiting or using that house as a place to preach, as he did at Matthew's, Simon's and Zaccheus' homes. Quite likely, it was Peter's home. Just after Jesus preached his first time in the local synagogue, Mark 1:29 reports that *"when they were come out of the synagogue, they entered into the house of Simon and Andrew, with James and John."* Now if Jesus practiced what he preached, he stayed there till he left. (See Mark 6:10) My point is: it cannot be stated as fact that Jesus owned or even rented a house. Nowhere else in the Bible can we find even the suggestion of Jesus living in a house or owning a home. What we do have here is a classic case of people wresting or twisting the scriptures for their own ends of justifying their excesses. (See II Peter 3:16)

If Jesus had had a house anywhere else besides Capernaum, it would surely have been in Jerusalem, where he visited many times. Yet we do not read of him staying in a house at all around Jerusalem, much less owning one there. Remember he had to borrow a place to have the last supper because he had no where to lay his head or set his table. About a week before Jesus died, he graciously accepted an invitation to dinner with Martha, Mary and Lazarus. Whether he spent the entire night there cannot be said with certainty. If he did, it was a rare exception that he slept indoors. I think it very likely that after dinner, Jesus and his disciples retired to the garden of Gethsemane. It seems that this was Jesus' custom. Judas, knowing this, was able to lead the band of soldiers there to arrest him. Jesus camped out in the garden of Gethsemane because he had nowhere to stay. In his ministry, The Son of man did indeed have no place to lay his head; at birth, he had only a makeshift manger; at his death, he had only a borrowed grave, because his rest was not in this world. When Jesus said he had nowhere to lay his head, that's exactly what he meant.

Matthew 19:27

Then answered Peter and said unto him, Behold, we have forsaken all, and followed you...

Further indication of the poverty and lowliness of Christ is that his apostles, who followed him, also lived that way. *"Even to this present hour, we both hunger and thirst, are naked and are buffeted, and have no certain dwelling place."* (I Corinthians 4:11) If the disciples were following a rich Jesus, they would have been buying houses and lands and living in motels like a rich Jesus would. But they did no such thing, even when large sums of money were later laid at their feet. A true follower of Jesus recognizes the merit of living as he did. Jesus did not live comfortably at the expense of or at the envy of anyone. He dwelt among us, not above us. The princes of the Gentiles may live wealthily at the expense of their subjects, but it is not so with our King.

Matthew 21:5-7

5. ***Tell ye the daughter of Zion, Behold, your King comes unto you, meek, and sitting upon an ass, and a colt, the foal of an ass.***
6. ***And the disciples went, and did as Jesus commanded them,***
7. ***And brought the ass, and the colt, and put on them their clothes, and they set him thereon.***

This was an astonishingly humble way for Jesus to make his entrance to Jerusalem. The thousands around him had the notion that he was ready to ascend to the throne of David. "*Hosanna to the Son of David!*" But as before, when people tried to "*take him by force, to make him a king*", he showed no interest. (See John 6:15) Jesus came to save us from our sins, a much greater enemy than Roman tyranny. Riding a colt into the city was about as lowly as Jesus could travel. Riding a horse, a camel, or in a chariot would have been more befitting of making a grand entrance. Yet Jesus, whose entire life was meek and humble, would have his formal presenting to Israel also meek and lowly. This was beautifully consistent with the rest of Christ's life and teaching.

Jesus came to save us from our sins,
a much greater enemy than Roman tyranny.

Mark 9:35

And he sat down, and called the twelve, and said unto them, if any man desire to be first, the same shall be last of all, and servant of all.

This does not sound like the mentality of someone who lives wealthily and has real estate around the country. If Jesus had said such a thing being rich, I imagine one of the disciples would have said, "But Jesus, you live rich." On the contrary, he who was meek and lowly of heart both taught and demonstrated those principles. Jesus made himself last of all by living lowlier than all, deferring to the needs and comforts of others before himself, and making himself a servant to many, whatever the cost to himself. There's no way it could be said that Jesus was last of all if he owned a number of homes, a luxury only a few can afford.

Mark 10:10

And in the house his disciples asked him again of the same matter.

This incident occurred in Judea on the east side of the Jordan. This was an area Jesus rarely visited. Yet we see Jesus and the disciples apparently staying in a house. Because the Holy Spirit does not deem it significant enough to elaborate, it remains an open question whether it was a rented house, a house where they were guests for the night or a house Jesus actually owned. However, we can deduce from the expression "*the house*" that it was not owned by Jesus or the apostles. If they had owned it, the expression would surely have read, "*their house.*" Most likely, based on similar accounts, they were guests in someone's house.

Mark 12:15

Shall we give, or shall we not give? But he, knowing their hypocrisy, said unto them, Why tempt ye me? Bring me a penny that I may see it.

Jesus is in the middle of one of his many confrontations with Pharisees. He needs a coin to make an illustration, but he does not have one. He literally does not have a penny to his name, or on his person.

Thus he must ask to borrow one from somebody. So often in the life of Jesus, we find him in need of such things as a borrowed crib, a borrowed boat — a borrowed penny, a borrowed donkey, borrowed linens and finally, a borrowed grave. I get the impression that Jesus intentionally kept himself poor and having need of bread daily. This allowed opportunity for people all around him to do him kindnesses, such as providing food, shelter, etc. We have similar opportunity to this day.

Mark 14:3-5

3. ***And being in Bethany in the house of Simon the leper, as he sat at meat, there came a woman, having an alabaster box of ointment of spikenard, very precious; and she broke the box, and poured the ointment on his head.***
4. ***And there were some that had indignation within themselves, and said, Why was this waste of the ointment made?***
5. ***For it might have been sold for more than three hundred pence, and have been given to the poor. And they murmured against her.***

Now this is a subtle point. The disciples, observing the woman doing an extravagant kindness, made objection to it, "*they murmured against her.*" If there had been other extravagances done for Jesus on occasion, this would not have seemed so objectionable to them. If Jesus and the disciples had been treated to lavish banquets or expensive penthouses, this would not have seemed so out of the ordinary. If Jesus had in any way lived the life of a wealthy man, they could hardly have had indignation at this incident. The very strong reaction expressed by some of the disciples indicates this was a one of a kind incident. What is said by the disciples in verse five is apparently what they were more accustomed to: money being spent not on themselves, but on the poor around them. This was such a common occurrence that when Jesus told Judas at the last supper, "*That thou doest, do quickly*", the disciples assumed he was being dispatched to "*give something to the poor.*" (John 13:27-29)

Mark 14:44

And he that betrayed him had given them a token (sign), saying, Whomsoever I shall kiss, that same is he; take him, and lead him away safely.

In most churches today, it would be easy to pick the preacher out of all the people in the church. Typically, he is the best dressed, most distinguished of those present. However, it was not so with Jesus and his disciples. His garb was as plain and typical as any man's. It was this very common appearance that made it so laughable to the Roman soldiers that he was a king. A short while later and they would mock him, "*Hail, King of the Jews!*" Isaiah foretold, "*There is no beauty that we should desire him*" or even distinguish him. (Isaiah 53:2) This was to teach us that "*the Lord sees not as man sees; for man looks on the outward appearance, but the Lord looks on the heart.*" (I Samuel 16:7)

Mark 15:43-46

43. ***Joseph of Arimathea, an honorable counselor, who also waited for the kingdom of God, came, and went in boldly unto Pilate, and craved (asked for) the body of Jesus.***
44. ***And Pilate marveled if he were already dead, and, calling unto him the centurion, he asked him whether he had been any while dead.***
45. ***And when he knew it from the centurion, he gave the body to Joseph.***
46. ***And he bought fine linen, and took him down, and wrapped him in the linen, and laid him in a sepulcher which had been hewn out of a rock, and rolled a stone unto the door of the sepulcher.***

Jesus had no estate which could subsidize the expense of his burial. Apparently, his occasional support during his ministry had also disappeared in the dark time of his death. When the Shepherd was struck, the flock was thoroughly scattered. Yet God raises up a man who will see to it that his son gets an honorable burial. Again, this kind of financial void was allowed in the life of Jesus so that others would have the privilege of supplying the need. It was common in Bible days that wealthy men would make provision for their burial by purchasing or constructing their grave in advance. (e.g., Abraham, Absalom, and this Joseph.) Even though Jesus knew months or years in advance, he made no provision for a grave, grave clothing, spices or any kind of funeral. This is not the way rich men depart, but it is how the poor usually do.

Luke 6:1

"And it came to pass...that he went through the corn fields; and his disciples plucked the ears of corn, and did eat rubbing them in their hands."

If Jesus was wealthy, he must have lost his credit card that day. The practice of the Jews helping themselves to their neighbors' crops was expressly allowed for the poor of the land. Ruth did the same thing and it was perfectly lawful. Not only did Jesus have no money to buy food himself, he apparently had no friend of means providing his needs at that time.

Notice they *"did eat rubbing them in their hands"*. Not only did they not have funds to buy food, they had no place to cook or were so famished they took no time to cook. Raw, hard corn right off the ears is pretty rough fare for a meal.

Luke 8:1-3

1. ***And it came to pass, afterward, that he went throughout every city and village, preaching and showing the glad tidings of the kingdom of God; and the twelve were with him,***
2. ***And certain women, who had been healed of evil spirits and infirmities: Mary, called Magdalene, out of whom went seven devils;***
3. ***And Joanna, the wife of Chuzas, Herod's steward; and Suzanna; and many others, who ministered unto him of their substance.***

Here, a group of well to do ladies accompanied Jesus and the disciples on a preaching tour. Notice these ladies are said to have ministered to Jesus of their substance. They would not have needed to do so if Jesus was independently wealthy as some claim. We do not hear of Jesus eating raw grain from the fields after this. However, we also do not see him traveling or living luxuriously or even what we would call comfortably. In the very next chapter, we find Jesus homeless as he travels extensively to preach the gospel. (See Luke 9:58.) So it is apparent that the ladies' support probably did no more than ensure that Jesus and his disciples ate well.

Of this passage, the great Bible commentator Matthew Henry writes, *"There were many of them that ministered to Christ of their substance. It was an instance (example) of the meanness (lowliness) of that condition to which our Savior humbled himself that he needed it, and of his great humility and condescension that he accepted it."* (Matthew Henry Commentary, Vol. 5, p. 657)[3]

This Laborer is especially worthy of his hire and this One who treads the corn should not be muzzled from eating the corn. The disciples and Jesus worked hard and the strain of the ministry was very taxing on them. Sometimes the constant pressure crowded out meal times. Sometimes the work left them so absolutely exhausted, they needed time away to recover. To a great degree, Jesus and the disciples, like Paul, ministered to their own necessities. Those so called ministers who idle away their hours, and seek more to be served than to serve are not worthy of "hire". Those who do neither good for themselves nor for others do not deserve support. It is the *laborer* who is worthy of hire, not the *laggard*.

Luke 9:7, 8

7. ***Now Herod, the tetrarch, heard of all that was done by him: and he was perplexed, because that it was said by some, that John was risen from the dead;***
8. ***And by some that Elijah had appeared; and by others, that one of the old prophets was risen again.***

The common opinion of who Jesus was is given here. Some had a silly, superstitious idea that John the Baptist had come back from the dead. This was the idea Herod latched onto, probably out of a guilty conscience. But notice the consistency of the others' opinion, that Jesus was Elijah, or one of the old prophets risen again. Though all of them were wrong, the most reasonable opinion was that Elijah had appeared, for it was predicted in Malachi 4:5 that Elijah would return.

What is interesting to our discussion here is the consistency of opinion most held. They nearly all regarded Jesus as one of the old prophets returned. Now people have a tendency to judge a great deal by appearance. It seems likely that the appearance, demeanor, and life style of Jesus reminded them a lot of the humble, poor life of the old prophets. We read that Elijah lived most of his life in the harsh desert wilderness, and that he wore a leather girdle. John the Baptist also lived a solitary life in the wilderness, wore a leather girdle and ate locusts and wild honey. You can't get much poorer than that. And yet the simple, humble life style of Jesus reminded most people of the prophets of old.

If Jesus had been staying in houses, frequenting the homes of the rich, wearing designer clothing and owned several houses, it is doubtful they would have thought him to be like the old prophets.

John 6:5,9,10

5. ***When Jesus then lifted up his eyes, and saw a great company come unto him, he said unto Philip, Where shall we buy bread, that these may eat?***
9. ***There is a lad here, who has five barley loaves and two small fishes; but what are they among so many?***
11. ***And Jesus took the loaves; and when he had given thanks, he distributed to the disciples..."***

This is, of course, the miracle of the loaves and fishes. The contents of one willing little boy's lunch, committed into Christ's hands, fed over 5,000 people. We may think that what we have to offer to God is insignificant, but when dedicated to him, our gift may do good beyond our farthest imagination.

Let's focus on Philip: he was given the unenviable task of providing dinner for the guests that day – all 5,000 of them. Philip checks around to see what food they have to offer. If Jesus, the apostles or Philip himself had had any food, he would certainly have mentioned theirs first to Jesus. It was only because they themselves were completely without food, that the boy's lunch came to attention. They would never have thought to give away someone else's food if they had not already given away their own, or had none to begin with. Either way, Jesus and company were a long way from the nearest Magic Market and had nothing to eat. The trip back home would have been a very hungry one.

We can be pretty sure that the *last* thing rich folks are going to do without is their food. They are loathe enough to part with their luxuries, but they would never do without food. This is clear evidence that Jesus and the apostles, far from wealthy, were frequently destitute. This was not a one time incident. At a later time, nearly the identical thing happened, except the second time, they fed over 4,000 with seven loaves and a few fish. Again, the disciples and Jesus apparently had no food. A third known incident was at a time when they had just crossed the sea of Galilee. Matthew 16:5 reports, *"And when his disciples were come to the other side, they had forgotten to take bread."* Whether by such forgetfulness or by lack of funds, Jesus and the disciples lived at a level of poverty that only a very few in the United States have ever seen.

Jesus and the disciples lived at a level of poverty that very few in the United States have ever seen.

John 19:23,24

23. ***Then the soldiers, when they had crucified Jesus, took his garments and made four parts, to every soldier a part; and also his coat. Now the coat was without seam, woven from the top throughout.***
24. ***They said therefore, among themselves, Let us not (tear) it, but cast lots for it, whose it shall be; that the scripture might be fulfilled, which says, They parted my raiment among them, and for my vesture they did cast lots. These things, therefore, the soldiers did.***

Some have called attention to the coat here and have said it was the equivalent of designer clothing. Yet there is nothing in this passage to say this. What can be said is that the coat was worth more than the other articles of clothing and that they could not make a fair division of loot with the coat in the mix. So they cast lots for it. I suspect that if the coat was of considerable value, the centurion in charge would have staked a claim on it. I find it impossible to believe that Jesus would wear designer grade clothing, because it would have been so incongruous with every other aspect of his life of humiliation. What I do find easy to believe is that men would put such a slant on this so as to make Jesus look like themselves, when they wear one and two thousand dollar suits. Promoting such nonsense encourages folks to splurge on purchases of fine clothing, buying expensive clothes just to be spending, routinely replacing entire lines of their wardrobe unnecessarily, squandering their income in satisfying their lust. What shall we say in that day when the Judge demands, "Why didn't you clothe me when I was naked?" Then we will answer him, "Lord, when did we see you naked?" He'll explain, "I was in those children dressed in threadbare, shabby clothing. You could have completely outfitted me with good clothes for the price of that one article of your extensive wardrobe."

John 19:26, 27

26. ***When Jesus, therefore, saw his mother, and the disciple standing by, whom he loved, he said unto his mother, Woman, behold your son!***
27. ***Then said he to the disciple, Behold your mother! And from that hour that disciple took her unto his own home.***

This is evidence that Jesus had no estate to leave to his mother and that he had no house in Jerusalem to bequeath her, as some claim. His only heritage was the affections and loyalties of his followers. It was a portion of this that he secured for his mother. How much better it was to receive a hundredfold sisters and brothers and sons and daughters, than houses and lands.

V. Conclusion

Did Jesus become rich in the ministry? No, he likely was poorer during his ministry than at any other time of his life. A lot of preachers know how that feels. No, he was not wealthy in the ministry, he was not wealthy growing up, he was not born into a wealthy family and it was prophesied that he would not be.

However, this is actually good news. Jesus became poor that we might be rich. All of his self denials and sufferings accrue to our benefit. *"For your sakes he became poor, that you through his poverty might be made rich."* (II Corinthians 8:9) He emptied himself that we might receive of his fullness. This is like the broke parents of a college student, who spend everything they have to keep their son in college. Every sacrifice and self denial of the parents provides benefit for the son.

Thus Jesus paid all and gave all for us. He laid aside his glory, humbled himself in becoming a man, the poorest of men, suffered death for our sakes, the most humiliating of deaths. All this results in unspeakable benefit to us! The shedding of his blood atones for our sins and we receive life more abundantly now in this time and in the world to come, eternal life.

> *"Jesus paid it all,*
> *All to him I owe;*
> *Sin had left a crimson stain,*
> *He washed it white as snow."*

"Freely you have received, freely give."

Matthew 10:8

What did Jesus Teach About Wealth?

Throughout the New Testament, there is conspicuous lack of attention given to wealth. You get the impression that the kingdom of God has little to do with money. The kingdom of God does not rise or fall on finances. Lack of finances does not hinder God's work, nor does plenty of it help much. Throwing a lot of money at a ministry or church does not make it grow. We've all seen spacious, fine facilities occupied by a sparse few. There are also works of God flourishing in borrowed building or in no building at all. Some have no funds at all, and yet are winning souls and strengthening disciples. The *only* necessary ingredients to successful Christianity are: God's grace and man's faith. Yet because money is so central to life on this planet, the subject does get some attention.

Now let's consider a few passages that illustrate Jesus' teaching on wealth. Does Jesus encourage us to work hard and get rich? Or does he teach us to be completely detached from money and the things of this world? Do different standards apply to itinerant preachers and fathers raising families? Let's hear it from the Master himself.

Matthew 5:40

And if any man will sue you at the law, and take away thy coat, let him have your cloak also.

Remember John the Baptist similarly exhorted, *"He that has two coats, let him impart (freely) to him that has none."* Here Jesus and John encourage a detachment of desire to the things of this world, easily letting go of them in rightful or wrongful cases. Remember Jonathan gave David his robe, his garments, his sword and his bow. How much more should we freely give who have freely received, and cheerfully so, since it is our Father's good pleasure to give us the kingdom! Doing so vividly testifies that we are not of this world.

Matthew 5:42

Give to him that asks of you, and from him that would borrow of (from) you, turn not...away.

As in verse 40, we are urged to easily relinquish our goods to forceful demands, so here we're exhorted to be easily entreated by humble requests. Our fleshly tendency is to turn away from requests for help, as the Levite who *"passed by on the other side."* We tend to turn a blind eye and a deaf ear to others' needs. But *"whoso stops his ears at the cry of the poor, he also shall cry himself, but shall not be heard."* (Proverbs 21:13) There are consequences to those who turn away from the poor: *"therefore to him that knows to do good, and does it not, to him it is sin."* (James 4:17)

Matthew 6:1,2

1. ***Take heed that you do not your alms before men, to be seen by them; otherwise you have no reward of your Father, who is in heaven.***

2. ***Therefore, when you do your alms, do not sound a trumpet before you, as the hypocrites do in the synagogues and in the streets, that they may have glory from men. Verily I say unto you, They have their reward.***

Jesus instructs us to give simply, without any fanfare or flourishing of trumpets. If we are recognized for our good, and it is reported on the five-o-clock news, or ends up in the newspaper or is publicized from the pulpit, we have already received reward enough, whether it was our idea or not.

Contrary to this teaching, "*Most men will proclaim every one his own goodness.*" (Proverbs 20:6) They have their reward. When we let on how Godly we are, how much we have been persecuted, how much we have suffered, or have been wrongly accused, the power of Christ no longer rests upon us. Rather, if we'd publicly declare our sins and faults so as to present ourselves in a lesser light to man, then our reward in heavenly places remains intact. The power of Christ rests on us and the person of Christ abides with us. This is our "*exceeding great reward*" and is a "*far more exceeding and eternal weight of glory.*"

Matthew 6:11
Give us this day our daily bread.

In this segment of the Lord's prayer we are encouraged to make request of our Father for our needs and comforts. And not in vain, for "*my God shall supply all (our) needs according to his riches in glory*" and sometimes our desires. Yet these verses do not at all justify our extravagance and ease. Very little do we find scripture moving us to ask of God for the goods of this world. Those who search the scriptures daily and thoroughly will see that these things are so. Usually, we're cautioned to the contrary, as in Matthew 6:19-21. (See chapter 4.)

Matthew 6:24

No man can serve two masters...you cannot serve God and mammon (money).

Many try, though they would probably deny it, "I'm not serving money; I serve only God." Oh really? If that's the case, then you would never miss church or a chance to serve the household of faith because of work commitments. "Well, I'd love to, Pastor, but I have to work this Saturday."

On the other hand, if a man was truly serving God more than money, we'd see him ready to forfeit income for the opportunity of rendering service to God. "Hi, Mr. Miller, I won't be in this Friday. I'm planning to help my church with Vacation Bible School."

Remember that Pilate was willing to defend Jesus until the chief priests starting meddling with his job. *"If you let this man go, you are not Caesar's friend...When Pilate therefore heard that saying, he brought Jesus forth, and sat down in the judgment seat..."* (John 19:12,13) Three verses later, Jesus was sentenced to be crucified. Too many of us are likewise fair weather friends of Jesus. We're willing to serve him until it meddles with our income.

Matthew 10:8

Freely you have received, freely give.

Nowhere in scripture do we see God's men receiving donations or gifts from people for whom they had done miracles. Samuel challenged, *"Whose ox have I taken?"* Naaman urged Elisha to accept the ten talents of silver and 6000 pieces of gold, a vast sum of money. Elisha refused. When Peter laid hands on the Samaritan Christians, they received the gift of the Holy Spirit. Then Simon, the ex-sorcerer, offered Peter money if he would lay hands on him to give him the same gift. Peter not very tactfully replied, *"Your money perish with you! Repent of this your wickedness...for I perceive that you are in the gall of bitterness and in the bond of iniquity."* (Acts 8: 20-23) This is not how preachers usually respond to offers of financial support. Peter likely had in mind, *"Freely you have received; freely give."*

Now please don't mis-apply this verse. It is perfectly proper for pastors and Christian workers to receive financial compensation for their labors. *"For the laborer is worthy of his hire."* Rather, it seems that when Jesus said *"freely give"*, he meant: do not accept pay for what God does. *God* heals the sick; *God* raises the dead. As far as we know, Jesus never accepted a donation from anyone he healed or raised from the dead. Neither should we. Yet the elders who rule well and labor in the word and doctrine or in any other work that benefits the household of faith are to *"be counted worthy of double honor"*. That is, double compensation. We cannot give too much to a good man of God.

Matthew 10:9,10

"Provide neither gold, nor silver, nor brass in your purses, Nor scrip (money holder) for your journey, neither two coats, neither shoes, nor yet staves: for the workman is worthy (deserving) of his meat."

This is part of the instructions Jesus gave to his twelve apostles when he sent them out to preach. Evidently, they took it quite literally, for long afterward they said, *"Silver and gold have I none"*.

Jesus' words were both an encouragement and a caution to those who give themselves to the ministry. The encouragement is that they would not have to go at their own expense. If they sow spiritual things, it is proper that they should reap carnal wages. (I Corinthians 9:11) They need not and must not provide their own gold and silver for their traveling expenses. Silver and gold they were to have none, but such as they had they would give: healing for the sick, cleansing for lepers, etc. They were to remain empty-handed so that the beneficiaries of their service would have opportunity to do kindness to them in return. The disciples were not to accept pay or gifts for their services, for freely they received, freely they must give. They were not to carry a scrip (wallet) as if they would accumulate funds. This way they must rely on God for their daily bread as did Israel in the wilderness and Elijah at the brook of Cherith. The Lord was to be their portion as with the Levites. Israel's manna would not keep more than a day. We thrive best spiritually when we depend on God daily. But if we have *"much goods laid up for many years"* we tend to be full and deny him and say *"Who is the Lord?"* (Luke 12:19, Proverbs 30:9)

In our prolific society, few of us know about daily dependence on our Father. We must come to realize that our security is in Jehovah-jireh and not in the abundance of the things which we possess.

Sometimes God takes a person away from the security of Egypt and sets him in the wilderness of uncertainty. If this sounds like you, God may be weaning you from reliance on the world and teaching you dependence on Him. See how God loves you?

Getting back to Matthew 10:9,10, it does not seem that Jesus meant this as general instructions for all Christians. Notice first: it is addressed to those in the ministry, for they are the *"workmen"*.

Second, it applies to those displaced from their homes, as the apostles were: *"for your journey"*. Jesus wanted his ambassadors to cast themselves on the hospitality of those whom they served, as the angels accepted Lot's hospitality and Abraham's dinner. This gives the host an opportunity to do a kindness to the Lord. *"Inasmuch as you have done it unto one of the least of these my brothers, you have done it unto me."*

Third, it seems to apply particularly to those who wield the mighty gifts of the Holy Spirit. Let those who receive such supernatural benefits gratefully care for the messengers of the benefits, as the jailer cared for Silas and Paul. Let not the messengers do this at their own expense.

Paul declined the support of the Corinthians: *"I kept myself from being burdensome to you."* (II Corinthians 11:9) Paul's own hands ministered to his necessities and to them that were with him. *"I have preached to you the gospel of Christ freely."* (II Corinthians 11:7) Paul wanted no room for accusation. Yet he acknowledges that he deprived the Corinthians the opportunity to support and care for him.

The expression *"the workman is worthy of his meat"* is well applied in financially supporting Christian workers and ministers that they may attend to their work without the distraction of another job. For a minister must not *"entangle himself with the affairs of this life that he may please him who has chosen to be a soldier"*. (II Timothy 2:4)

Matthew 13:22

"He also that received seed among the thorns is he that hears the word; and the care of this world, and the deceitfulness of riches, choke the word, and he becomes unfruitful."

You might recognize this as part of the parable of the sower and the seed. The soil where this seed landed was actually fertile ground. That was part of the problem. Notice *everything* grew there: good seed and thorns. The good seed grew to some degree of maturity, but stopped short of producing fruit. The problem was that too much was growing in the same place. The same spot of ground cannot support good seed and thorns, just as a man cannot serve God and money.

Maybe you're such fertile ground as this. You can do anything – and try to do everything. You thrive on challenges. You volunteer a lot. When you put your heart into a project, team, organization or business, it prospers. You love to shoulder responsibility and do good. That's exactly the problem. You get so distracted doing good that you neglect to do the one needful thing. You have Martha syndrome, "*Martha, Martha, you are careful (care-filled) and troubled about many things.*"

Hard working Marthas need to be careful of letting thorns grow in their good ground. Their fertile minds belong to the Master and are properly employed only in producing fruit for Him. "*Whatsoever you do in word or deed, do all in the name of the Lord Jesus, giving thanks to God and the Father by him.*" (Colossians 3:17)

Matthew 16:24-26

"Then said Jesus unto his disciples, If any man will come after me, let him deny himself, and take up his cross, and follow me.
For whoever will save his life shall lose it: and whoever will lose his life for my sake shall find it.
For what is a man profited, if he shall gain the whole world, and lose his own soul?"

We are here taught to take up our cross, for we are to be "*crucified with Christ*" and must "*die daily*" as Paul. Notice this is a self-imposed discipline: "*let him (or her) deny himself*". We are to deny ourselves not just for the sake of denying, but in order to take up our cross. Let's be willing to let go of our comforts, our plans, our positions in order to perform the ministry or service God appoints for us. Even if our plans were to gain for us so much as a world of wealth, it would be small compensation for the loss of our soul. The truth is, if we have our heart set on building our own kingdom of wealth or feathering our own nest with comforts, we are already in danger of forfeiting our own soul. For "*if any man loves the world, the love of the Father is not in him.*"

It is not wholesome for us to so live for self. If we live only for the purpose of pampering or providing for ourselves, we corrupt our soul. "*Whosoever will save his life shall lose it.*" However, if we are willing to lose ourselves in the cause of Christ and in the care of his household, we shall find our life. Not just eternal life, but abundant life now in this time.

In his wisdom/kindness, God has set deterrents before us to keep us from becoming too indulgent. If we overeat, we get fat. If we get drunk, we get hangovers. If we overload on pleasure, we experience withdrawal or disgust.

Likewise, he has set up rewards for us if we deny ourselves for his sake. A special inner joy is for those who give of themselves to others. Consider Isaiah 58:10 in the NASB, *"And if you give yourself to the hungry, and satisfy the desire of the afflicted, then your light will rise in darkness, and your gloom will become like midday."* This sort of scriptural promise is better insurance against hard times than an investment portfolio. The person who forgets himself and is preoccupied with others' needs is promised that their light will rise in dark times and that their gloomy times will become as bright as midday.

A woman once announced to her pastor that she was planning to have a nervous breakdown the following week. The wise pastor said he was sorry to hear that, but hoped that it would go well. Then he said, "Before you do, would you help me with a couple of problems?" She replied, "Of course, Pastor, I'd be glad to help." The pastor told her of a single mother who was ill at the time and was not able to cook. He asked the woman if she would please prepare a meal and bring it over to the family. She said she'd be glad to. The pastor also asked if she would bring some home-made cookies to a certain elderly woman to cheer her up. Again the woman said she would. A couple of weeks later the pastor called her and asked how the nervous breakdown went. She said, "I haven't had time for it. I've been too busy." "What have you been so busy with", he asked. She answered happily, "I've had to do shopping for Mrs. Broward (the elderly woman). She doesn't drive, you know. And I've been helping Nancy with the kids and housework every day. But she's getting better." "You sound like you're in a good mood." "Pastor, I haven't been so happy in years."

You see, God has so "wired" us that we feel more blessed when we give than when we receive. If we lose our lives for others, we find the happiest life possible.

Matthew 19:16,21,22
"And, behold, one came and said to him, Good Master, what good thing shall I do, that I may have eternal life?...
Jesus said to him, If you will be perfect, go and sell that you have, and give to the poor, and you shall have treasure in heaven: and come and follow me.
But when the young man heard that saying, he went away sorrowful: for he had great possessions."

It is strange indeed that the very thing which we were sure would make us happy, in the end will pierce us through with many sorrows. (I Timothy 6:10) How many in America are like this man:

a. He rightly comes to Christ.
b. He has a good heart.
c. He seeks eternal life.
d. He is wealthy and in a position to do a lot of good, as Cornelius, who "*gave much alms to the people*" or the other centurion who built a synagogue for the Jews.
e. He is a religious, well mannered fellow who would have been voted "most likely to go to heaven."
f. Jesus likes the man. In Mark's account of this incident, he reports, "*Then Jesus beholding him loved him*".

All this would seem to indicate the man was a believer and would go to heaven. Yet he fell short. He knew it himself, for he said, *"What lack I yet?"* Jesus also laments his unhappy state, *"A rich man shall hardly enter into the kingdom of heaven."* Why? Because it is so excruciatingly difficult for a rich man to let go of his wealth. His possessions and assets are so cherished and beloved to him that it is a near hopeless case to dislodge his (or her) affection from it. If a fool and his money are soon parted, then it's a greater fool who refuses to part with his money for the saving of his soul.

Matthew 19:27, 28
"Then answered Peter and said unto him, Behold, we have forsaken all and followed thee; what shall we have therefore?" And Jesus said unto them, Verily I say unto you, that you which have followed me, in the regeneration when the Son of man shall sit in the throne of his glory, you also shall sit upon twelve thrones, judging the twelve tribes of Israel."

Here Jesus teaches, in general, that sacrifices and faithfulness in this life are compensated in the next. But notice some important details: first, that Peter's reflection reveals a poor motive. "Lord, look what we've done. What are we going to get out of this?" His question focuses on his personal sacrifice and he seems to expect reward on the basis of his sacrifice. Now notice how wisely Jesus words his response: *"You which have followed me"* shall have reward. Reward is not necessarily given to those who have forsaken all (or some). Sacrifices made for the wrong motives are not rewarded. *"And though I bestow all my goods to feed the poor...and have not charity, it profits me nothing."* Those who follow Jesus shall have reward. Those who make sacrifices, who leave all *in order to* follow Jesus or *in obedience to* Jesus, shall have reward. However, an arbitrary bestowing of goods or giving away of possessions for the purpose of reward constitutes a poor motive and warrants no reward. Jesus had just told the rich man to give to the poor and *"come and follow me"*, and he would have treasure in heaven. If he only gave to the poor and not follow Jesus, no deal. This excludes philanthropism and charitable works as tickets to heaven. The Bible could not be clearer on this point. The gift of eternal life is granted *"not by works of righteousness which we have done, but according to his mercy."* (Titus 3:5) Holding the notion that we may achieve eternal life in heaven by kindness, generosity and quality living shows that we have a cheapened view of heaven. Remember the millionaire who spent about seven million dollars for a few days visit to the Mir Space Station? Well imagine if God offered one week visits to heaven. What would such a trip go for? A billion dollars? One hundred billion? Yet God does not offer a one week tour package. It's eternity or nothing. How do you put a price on even five minutes of perfect bliss, much less an eternity? Eternal joy in heaven is too costly to purchase, too high to merit. It is so precious and priceless that it may be conveyed to us only as a gift.

This is like the pearl diver who had long been good friends with a missionary. When the missionary announced to the pearl diver his plans to retire and return to his home country, the pearl diver was deeply moved. As an expression of his love to the missionary, the pearl diver presented him his most prized possession: the largest and finest pearl he had ever seen. The missionary gasped with admiration and disbelief. He stammered, "I – I don't know what to say." The pearl was worth enough to retire either man for life. Thinking quickly, the missionary said, "I must pay you for this. I'll give you my life savings." The pearl diver was offended at the suggestion. Again the missionary offered, "I'll give you my life savings and all my possessions." Again the pearl diver was annoyed and said, "Sir this pearl is priceless. You cannot buy it. You must accept it as a gift or you cannot have it at all." At this the missionary accepted the pearl and said, "Hear me, my friend. All these years I have preached to you of God's offer of forgiveness and eternal life. Yet you have said you were a good man and that you would surely enter heaven because of it. You are doing as I have just done: trying to pay for the gift that has been offered to you freely. Yet God's gift is as this pearl: priceless. You must accept it as a gift or you cannot have it at all." The pearl diver finally understood and, as the story goes, accepted the gift of God that day.

How about you, dear friend? Are you making the same mistake the pearl diver did? You intended to please God with your good life and merit your way to heaven. Yet you unwittingly offend God, just as the missionary offended the pearl diver. God's offer of eternal life and the forgiveness of sin is so vastly valuable, that we may have it only as a gift.

Matthew 21:12, 13

"And Jesus went into the temple of God, and cast out all them that sold and bought in the temple, and overthrew the tables of the moneychangers, and the seats of them that sold doves,
And said unto them, It is written, My house shall be called the house of prayer; but you have made it a den of thieves."

This is about the only time Jesus displayed fiery action or emotion. He expresses the Father's righteous resentment against those who corrupt his courts with "*filthy lucre*". Notice several lessons. First, we may be sure that Jesus is keenly observant of all that transpires in the house of God; even to the discerning of the thoughts and intents of the heart. Recall the widow's mites. He sees not only as man sees, that is, the outward, orderly appearance of seats and tables; but also the inward crookedness of men's hearts. He who is full of eyes within and without, sees whether the minister (of all people) in the sanctuary (of all places) has his heart on the wealth in the church or on God's word *to* the church. It is an abomination to the Almighty that when men are in the house of God, they would ponder their possessions rather than his person, and savor their savings more than their Savior. Even in church we can become so fixated on finances, that it requires a scourge to drive it from our minds. This is putting an abomination of desolation in a holy place. Those who do so are *"cast out"*. What happens to the finances we improperly set our affections on in the house of God? It is *"overthrown"*. It was a judgment of God when King Hezekiah cut the gold off the doors and pillars of the temple to give to the invading Assyrians. Likewise when the shields of gold were taken from King Rehoboam. When money and gold lure away our affections from God, He is likely to remove it for our safety.

Matthew 22:21

"...Then said he unto them, Render therefore unto Caesar the things that are Caesar's; and unto God the things that are God's."

You may recall that these words are Jesus' response to the Pharisees' trick question: "Should we pay the tax to Caesar or not?" Clearly, the answer was "yes". Jesus himself paid taxes. In Matthew 17:24-27, he directs Peter to pay a certain tax for the two of them.

The lesson here seems to be: fulfill all financial obligations, whether civil, religious or personal. Those who fail to do so are unjust. If a man refuses to pay his proper tax, or tithe, he is not rendering to Caesar his due or to God his due. Both Caesar (the government) and God provide much good for us, and therefore should get their due. If a Christian gets ahead financially at the expense of either of these, his gold shall be witness against him.

Matthew 25:14-30

14. ***"For the kingdom of heaven is as a man traveling into a far country, who called his own servants, and delivered unto them his goods.***
15. ***And unto one he gave five talents, to another two, and to another one; to every man according to his several ability; and straightway took his journey.***
16. ***Then he that had received the five talents went and traded with the same, and made them five other talents.***
17. ***And likewise he that had received two, he also gained other two.***
18. ***But he that had received one went and dug in the earth and hid his lord's money.***
19. ***After a long time the lord of those servants comes, and reckons with them.***
20. ***And so he that had received five talents came and brought other five talents, saying, Lord, you delivered to me five talents: behold, I have gained beside them five talents more.***
21. ***His lord said unto him, Well done thou good and faithful servant: you have been faithful over a few things, I will make you ruler over many things: enter thou into the joy of thy lord.***
22. ***He also that had received two talents came and said, Lord, you delivered to me two talents: behold I have gained two other talents beside them.***
23. ***His lord said unto him, Well done, good and faithful servant; you have been faithful over a few things, I will make you ruler over many things: enter thou into the joy of thy lord.***

24. *Then he which had received the one talent came and said, Lord, I knew you that you are a hard man, reaping where you have not sown, and gathering where you have not (strewn):*
25. *And I was afraid, and went and hid thy talent in the earth: lo, there you have (what) is yours.*
26. *His lord answered and said unto him, You wicked and slothful servant, you knew that I reap where I sowed not, and gather where I have not (strewn):*
27. *You ought therefore to have put my money to the exchangers, and then at my coming I should have received mine own with usury.*
28. *Take therefore the talent from him, and give it unto him which has ten talents.*
29. *For unto everyone that has shall be given, and he shall have abundance: but from him that hath not shall be taken away even that which he has.*
30. *And cast ye the unprofitable servant into outer darkness: there shall be weeping and gnashing of teeth."*

This well known parable is laden with lessons. In general, we are here exhorted to be good stewards of what God has given us. Has God blessed us with a good upbringing? Then let us rear our children well. Has God blessed us with good knowledge of His word? Let us faithfully minister the word to others. Has God blessed us with financial means? Let *"every man according to his several ability"* minister to the furtherance of his kingdom.

Corollary truths relevant to our topic may also be found here. Notice in verse 14 who owns the *"goods"* or *"talents"*: not the ones who had it in their possession, but their lord. Likewise with us. We are simply stewards of what is in our possession. God is the owner. Not just the tenth is the

Lord's, but the total. We should present our tithe to the Lord and yet consider that our homes, vehicles and boats also belong to him. Those also should be used for His honor.

Not just the tenth is the Lord's, but the total.

One well-to-do Sunday school teacher uses his yacht for soul-winning opportunities and for promoting attendance in his class.

A Christian physician hosts annual Christian jamborees at his ranch in Gulfport, Mississippi. Another believer, instead of driving around in a luxury vehicle, bought a fifteen passenger van so that he could haul that many neighborhood kids to church. To these men, it all belongs to God.

The question is: how much return is our Lord getting for the investments he entrusted to us? One wealthy man contributed $100,000.00 to the bus ministry of First Baptist Church of Hammond, Indiana. With his help, the church leases about 200 buses every Sunday to deliver an average of 10,000 people to church. Every Sunday, a number of these people become Christians. Very likely, the owner paid his tithe on the $100,000.00 when he earned it. Yet he considered the principle also belonged to God. Once in a while, we should give like a king.

Next we see that the lord gave something to every servant mentioned. (v. 15) We may assume that no servant was left empty-handed. It is certainly so with us that God has given all of us varying measures of ability and assets. Let no one think they have nothing of any value to God. Remember that when God called Moses he had nothing but a stick in his hand. The question is: *"What is that in your hand?"*

In verse 16, the servants traded and gained for their master. However, many *"trade"* today and make gain only for themselves. Trading for our Master's gain results in the increase of *His* kingdom, not ours. *"What things were gain to me, those I counted loss for Christ."* (Philippians 3:7)

If God has prospered us financially, let us not say, *"I will pull down my barns and build greater"*. Rather, let us invest wisely in ministries which bring a good return for our Master. This would include ministries that are winning souls, building up new believers or meeting urgent personal needs in the name of Christ. *"Whatsoever you do in word or deed, do all in the name of the Lord Jesus."* (Colossians 3:17)

Now notice in verse 18 that the third servant *"dug in the earth, and hid his lord's money."* We see that his investing *"in the earth"* resulted in no gain. Let us beware of a similar error. Investing in the things of this world is hiding our Lord's money. This is what some churches and associations do which invest savings in the stock market or bonds. Such investing in the earth accomplishes nothing for their Master. Some might object, "But the savings grew twenty percent in two years. Now we have more to put into the church or mission work." Yet it could be countered that the kingdom gained nothing in the two years. Suppose the same sum had rather been invested in turning a bi-vocational pastor into a full time minister. The likely result is that several souls may have been won for the kingdom of God, the household of faith better edified and the church strengthened and increased. How much better to sow carnal things and reap spiritual things!

Verse 19 delivers the sobering truth that our Lord shall reckon with us. *"For we must all appear before the judgment seat of Christ; that every one may receive the things done in his body...whether it be good or bad."* (II Corinthians 5:10) We see by the master's dialogue with his servants that he expects, or rather demands, gain for his kingdom from each one. All of us must be profitable servants. None are exempted. Even if our skill or offering seems paltry to us, our Master expects us to produce. Let each be faithful, whether a widow presenting two mites, or shepherds giving but simple worship, or a broker giving vast sums.

Matthew 26: 6-13

6. ***"Now when Jesus was in Bethany, in the house of Simon the leper,***
7. ***There came unto him a woman having an alabaster box of very precious ointment, and poured it on his head, as he sat at meat.***
8. ***But when his disciples saw it, they had indignation, saying, To what purpose is this waste?***
9. ***For this ointment might have been sold for much, and given to the poor.***
10. ***When Jesus understood it, he said unto them, Why trouble ye the woman? For she has wrought a good work upon me.***
11. ***For you have the poor always with you; but me you have not always.***
12. ***For in that she poured this ointment on my body, she did it for my burial.***
13. ***Verily I say unto you, Wherever this gospel shall be preached in the whole world, there shall also this, that this woman hath done, be told for a memorial of her."***

Jesus takes the occasion of a woman's kindness to give us some powerful principles.

First, we cannot be too extravagant in honoring Christ our King. Maybe Solomon was a bit extravagant with his twelve lions of gold. Maybe we overdo it with Super Bowl extravaganzas or Miss America pageants. But we may safely ascribe all *"blessing, and honor, and glory, and power, unto him that sits upon the throne and unto the Lamb for ever and ever."* (Revelation 5:13) It would be difficult to overstate any attribute of Christ or overdo any honor to him. Too often, Christ gets only our pocket change and spare time. How pleasant to occasionally see someone who gives Him all or gives Him their best! Abel gave the "*firstlings*", the best, of his flock, while today we give discarded clothes. Hannah gave her first-born child to the Lord; today we give our children to soccer, school events and music training at the Lord's expense.

May God raise up among us men and women sold out to him, who divide their loyalty to no other. First, God must have our hearts, then our service will have no bounds. Our thought will no longer be, "Am I supposed to tithe on my net income or my gross income?" The question becomes, "Can I give an extra hundred this week?"

In the days of the apostles, folks sold houses and land, giving the entire proceeds to God's work, not just the tithe. Every Christian ought to try that once. Let's learn to give offerings of a pleasing aroma to Him.

Oseola McCarty, of Hattiesburg, Mississippi, worked much of her life doing laundry work for college students. She lived very frugally, saving her money, a dollar today, maybe two the next day. Eventually at retirement she had saved up $168,000.00. She ended up giving *all* her savings to the University of Southern Mississippi to set up a scholarship fund for deserving young ladies.

C. T. Studd was the number one ranked cricket player in England in 1882 and in 1883. A national hero, Studd became a Christian, and later went to China as a missionary, leaving behind a career as a famous and popular professional athlete. In 1887, he inherited approximately 33,000 British pounds, a vast sum probably worth well over a couple of million dollars in today's money. Acting on the passage in Acts, *"all that believed sold their possessions and goods and parted them to all men, as every man had need"*, Studd gave away virtually all his wealth. He gave 5000 pounds to Dwight Moody, who used the money to start the Moody Bible Institute in Chicago. Another 5000 pounds resulted in fifty missionaries being sent out in India. Other large sums of money were sent to the relief of poor folk in London, the support of George Mũller's orphans and to the China Inland Mission. He reserved 3400 pounds to give to his newly wed wife for setting up a household for them. However, she gave away all that amount, citing the verse where Jesus told the rich man, *"sell all that you have and distribute unto the poor."* [4] Now it's your turn.

Second, we must give with a good heart. Though the woman was criticized for not giving wisely, Jesus both defended and commended her. He looked not so much on the outward appearance as on her heart. He saw her love and gratitude and that was a more pleasing fragrance to him than the spikenard.

Third, lavish kindnesses to the poor are proper. Notice Jesus did not criticize the criticizers, either. He let stand their word, *"this ointment might have been sold for much and given to the poor"*. He could have said, "Now hold it right there! We can't be giving that much to the poor." Jesus in fact regards such kindnesses done to the poor, to the least of these, as done to him. *"You have done it unto me."*

How many of us have precious ointment or possessions in our homes which could be sold for much and given to the poor. Maybe someone reading this has a diamond pendant or a genuine pearl necklace worth thousands of dollars. Consider what you could do for that struggling single mother. You might be able to provide the down payment on a home for them and situate them for life. "But you have no idea how much sentimental value it has to me!" Then your gift will have the fragrance of spikenard.

Someone else may have gold coins, priceless antiques or prized collections they could part with. The proceeds may be committed toward paying for dental work for a hurting child, providing a reliable car for the pastor's wife, covering the tuition for a promising young Christian or paying off the church building note. In some cases, the sacrifice may be painful; remember the vial of spikenard had to be broken.

Fourth, extravagant works for the Lord are never forgotten. *"This shall be told for a memorial of her."* First, the Lord never forgets. *"God is not* *unrighteous to forget your work and labor of love."* Not only do our works follow us to our heavenly reward, but God remembers our works to our benefit in this life. Cornelius' alms came up for a memorial to God and so do yours. Second, people will never forget. We don't remember all the little good things we've ever done. (It's probably good that we don't.) Yet we *can* remember the big things we do. For the rest of our life, the recollection of one of those big things can install a smile on our face and joy in our heart. Third, others will never forget. John adds the detail that *"the house was filled with odor of the ointment"*. Everyone around found the good work to be of a pleasant fragrance. We should not advertise our own good as the unbelievers do. *"Most men will proclaim every one his own goodness."* Rather, we are exhorted, *"let not your left hand know what your right hand does"*. Let every man see to the performing of good works and let God see to the publicizing of them. When word of it begins to circulate, maybe others will be provoked unto like good works.

Matthew 26:14-16

14. ***"Then one of the twelve, called Judas Iscariot, went unto the chief priests,***
15. ***And said unto them, What will you give me, and I will deliver him unto you? And they covenanted with him for thirty pieces of silver.***
16. ***And from that time, he sought opportunity to betray him."***

See to what depths of darkness the love of money will drive a man! It is engraved in stone *"thou shalt not covet"*. Yet this Jew says *"what will you give me"*. The prodigal son first says, *"Father, give me"*. Judas is not the only one to betray his Master for a few pieces of silver. Businessmen compromise the principles of Christ to undercut the competition. Others once close to Christ betray him by circumventing the law and bringing a bad name on Christians. Even ministers can lose their first love and become more enamored with wealth and prestige, betraying him who called them. This seems to be the error of Judas, the Zealot. He probably had in mind a prominent position in a new Messianic kingdom along with wealth and ease. How easily we come to *"savor not the things that be of God, but the things that be of men"*.

Even ministers can lose their first love and become more enamored with wealth and prestige, betraying him who called them.

Matthew 27:3-5

3. ***Then Judas, which had betrayed him, when he saw that he was condemned, repented himself, and brought again the thirty pieces of silver to the chief priests and elders,***
4. ***Saying, I have sinned in that I have betrayed the innocent blood. And they said, What is that to us? See thou to that.***
5. ***And he cast down the pieces of silver in the temple, and departed, and went and hanged himself.***

Behold the wages of sin. Here is another who, for the love of money, erred from the faith and pierced himself through with sorrow. The pleasures of sin are but for a season; in Judas' case, a very short season. His reward of iniquity lasted about as long as the wealth and honor bestowed by Emperor Belshazzar on Godly Daniel.

We do not realize the results of our sins and misplaced values. Sin brings us farther than we intended to go, costs us more than we intended to pay, and keeps us longer than we intended to stay. How many in the end say as Judas might have said, "I didn't think it would come to this".

Judas *"brought again the thirty pieces of silver to the chief priests"*. For the revenues of a compromised life are so far from satisfying. The internal guilt can be so expensive that we wish we could go back and undo our wrongs. Zaccheus would agree.

Mark 6:1

"Is not this the carpenter, the son of Mary?"

Jesus was a winsome man and extremely brilliant. Luke reports that *"Jesus increased in wisdom and ...in favor with God and man"*. At the age of twelve, he awed the Ph.D.s of his time with his wisdom. He was a child prodigy. As an adult, he debated the best minds in Israel and never lost. He was also very well liked. Sinners and saints flocked to him, no doubt, because they sensed that he loved them.

Jesus was the epitome of a motivational speaker and had a charismatic ability to lead and organize. He could have gone to the top of any profession he chose. He'd have been an ideal C.E.O. He could have been the wealthiest merchant alive or a cattleman of unprecedented success. This *"greater than Solomon"* could have been richer than Solomon. He could easily have been king in Israel. Yet at the prospect of being vaulted to the throne of Israel, he said (more or less), "No thanks."

Well what profession did he choose? The carpentry business. His choice obviously had nothing to do with the money in it. I rather think he chose it for its usefulness to others. This would follow his own words, *"whoever will be chief among you, let him be your minister (server)"*.

Now what does this teach us about wealth? Simply this: that opportunity for wealth should not be the basis for choosing our vocation; but rather, how much good we can do for others.

A Christian woman in New Orleans impressed me when she said she was leaving the law profession to teach grade school. She felt that law professionals aren't doing society any good (an opinion I share), and that she'd be helping more people as a teacher.

How about you? Is your profession a pool of sharks trying to eat each other? What will be your legacy at retirement? A long trail of victims, suckers and exploited pawns? Happy memories.

On the other hand, if you choose a profession and lifestyle of serving, giving good measure and benefiting others, you could have a legacy more like that of Dorcas. *"Now there was at Joppa a certain disciple... called Dorcas: this woman was full of good works and almsdeeds which she did ... Then Peter arose and went with them. When he was come ... all the widows stood by him weeping, and showing the coats and garments which Dorcas made while she was with them."* (Acts 9:36, 39)

God forbid that Christians would stoop to work for a casino, lounge, liquor distributor or an ungodly man, with the flimsy excuse, "Well it pays better."

Mark 8:36

"For what shall it profit a man, if he shall gain the whole world, and lose his own soul?"

So many seem to be trying to gain the whole world. And the likelihood is that they will lose their soul in the process. Somebody needs to get the message: "you *can't* have it all". Even if you did, where would you put it?

Well, just what would a man profit if he were to gain the whole world? The truth is, plenty, but for just a little while. Eventually, the bill comes due. All the pleasures of sin are but for a season.

Years ago, an acquaintance of mine named Jack won a $250,000 settlement for injuries sustained in a fire. About a week later, he ended up in jail where he began serving a six year sentence. He had all that money but was unable to enjoy it.

So many of us get so caught up in the pleasure of the process of acquisition, that we are powerless to enjoy what we have. We have a miserly obsession for counting our wealth and watching it grow. If we neglect our soul in the meantime, it will one day be said also to us, *"Thou fool, this night your soul shall be required of you."* When we stand before the Judge, it will matter little whether we had gained hundreds or millions of dollars.

Of all people, Christians should grasp the concept that life is less like a game of poker than a game of rummy: the object of the game is to end up empty-handed. If you have too much at the end, it actually counts against you. *"Your gold and silver is cankered; and the rust of them shall be a witness against you."* (James 5:3)

One peasant woman in Guatemala had the right idea. She was told she would die of cancer within a few months. When missionaries arrived at her home to pray for her, they found her alone and her house completely empty. She had given everything away. She had the joy of seeing her possessions make others happy *before* she died. How about you? Why do we cling so tenaciously to our possessions as if we will have them forever? Are we as foolish as the pharaohs? I have yet to see a U-haul following behind a hearse.

"What shall it profit a man if he shall gain the whole world and lose his own soul?" What constitutes losing one's own soul? When a man becomes so allured at the prospect of wealth that the hope of it is continually on his mind, he has lost his soul. When a man is so obsessed with gain, that he compulsively rakes in more and more, far beyond what he needs, he has lost his soul. Typically, such a man also loses interest in God, in the Bible, in his church and sometimes, even in his family. That man loses out even in this life. He takes pleasure in things that do not satisfy very well or very long.

Certainly a man can come into a great deal of gain *without* abandoning principle or neglecting his God. However, it shall be harder for him than if he lived more moderately. Wealth is a hazard which few escape unscathed. *"They that will* (to) *be rich fall into temptation and a snare."*

Mark 10:28-30

"Then Peter began to say unto him, 'Lo, we have left all and have followed you.'

And Jesus answered and said, 'Verily, I say unto you, There is no man that has left house, or brothers, or sisters, or father, or wife, or children, or lands, for my sake, and the gospel's,

But he shall receive a hundredfold now in this time, houses, and brothers and sisters, and mothers, and children, and lands, with persecutions; and in the world to come eternal life."

This same incident was reported in Matthew, but Mark adds more detail, to which we will give attention. In Matthew, Jesus' answer addresses more the rewards of discipleship in the next life. Mark gives more that part of Jesus' answer which confirms reward in this life. Jesus confirms to us that those who sacrifice or suffer loss for the gospel's sake *"shall receive a hundredfold now in this time."* Our reward is not entirely in the next life. The nice part about God rewarding us in this life is that it is always a pure, sweet reward. Sometimes, worldly gain is bittersweet, or comes with strings attached and is usually taxed. Not so with the gift of God. He gives in good measure and in perfect timing. Besides supplying our daily bread, He blesses us *"with all spiritual blessings"* from *"heavenly places"*. For our carnal, menial service, God endows us with *"riches in glory by Christ Jesus"*. We may sow carnal things and reap spiritual things. Pity the man whose only reward is the base things of this life. Pity more the man who desires no more.

Mark 11:2,3

"(Jesus) says unto them, 'Go your way into the village over against you: and as soon as you be entered into it, you shall find a colt tied, whereon never man sat; loose him and bring him.

And if any man say unto you, Why do you this? say ye that the Lord has need of him; and straightway he will send him hither."

Jesus is about to make his triumphal entry into Jerusalem. He sends these two disciples to bring him a colt to ride on into the city. Exactly as he had prophesied, the disciples are first challenged and then permitted to take the colt. It is very likely the owner who addresses them. It is also very likely that the colt was later returned.

Now if the disciples had been told to first ask the owner, we probably never would have heard of this incident. It is because this seems so out of character for Jesus that Scripture makes note of it. Jesus must have known that such an appearance of presumption on his part would be disturbing to some of his followers. Yet he goes through with it anyway because the accompanying lessons are invaluable.

This is purely conjecture on my part, but I would not be surprised if the colt was the donkey's firstborn. (We learn from Zechariah 9:9 that the colt was a donkey.) If that were the case, then Exodus 13:1,2 would apply, *"And the Lord spoke unto Moses saying, Sanctify unto me all the firstborn, whatsoever opens the womb among the children of Israel, both of man and of beast: it is mine."* Here, God's ownership is by virtue of redemption, because He redeemed Israel from Egyptian annihilation. He could reasonably stake a claim of ownership to all Israel (and all that Israel owned), because he saved their lives. To the victor goes the spoil. When Abram (Abraham) defeated the armies of King Chedorlaomer, rescuing several other kings, the king of Sodom said, *"take the goods of thyself"*. (Genesis 14:21) He was acknowledging Abraham's right of ownership by redemption.

So if the colt was the first born, Jesus (being the redeemer of Israel) could lawfully say, *"It is mine."* Likewise for those of us among the Gentiles whom Jesus has redeemed from sin, he becomes rightful owner of us by redemption. And what a very insignificant thing it is to add that he is also rightful owner of what we have! When the fiancée purchases the $10,000.00 engagement ring, no one questions whether he should own the velvet box it comes in.

Jesus has an additional basis of ownership to the colt by being Creator. Being one person of the Godhead, he is co-creator of everything that is made. (John 1:3) This is the same premise of ownership expressed in Ezekiel 18:4, *"Behold, all souls are mine"*. This is a far more universal right of ownership than that of redemption. For redemption applies only to a few. Ownership by being creator applies to all. Again we may also reckon ourselves to be debtors to God as being His creations and as being sustained by him.

We belong to God because He created us and we are doubly God's if He is also our Redeemer. We do not lend our colt to God; He lends His colt to us. Likewise with all that we have. When Hannah delivered little Samuel to Eli, she said, *"I have lent him to the Lord"*. But actually, God lent Samuel to her. We are stewards of all God's goods that are in our care. It is not our vineyard. It has been *"let out"* to us and we are to cultivate its use for our Master's gain. (Mark 12:1,2)

We may learn one more principle from Jesus making his grand entrance into Jerusalem not in a gilded chariot, or on a royal litter, or on a noble stallion, or on an economy mule, or even on a humble little donkey. Rather, he came to Jerusalem as he came to Bethlehem, meek and lowly. He was born where even the poorest would disdain to be born – in a stable! He rode upon that which, I suppose, even the poorest would not. It would probably have been more honorable for Jesus to stride in on foot, than to ride on a clumsy, inexperienced bony little colt. This would be the equivalent of a world class evangelist due to speak at a city-wide campaign and arriving on a bicycle. Those who choose to arrive honorably in limousines, I suppose find correspondingly less honor in the pulpit.

Mark 12:41-44

"And Jesus sat over against the treasury, and beheld how the people cast money into the treasury: and many that were rich cast in much.

And there came a certain poor widow, and she threw in two mites, which make a farthing.

And he called unto him his disciples, and said unto them, Verily I say unto you, That this poor widow has cast more in, than all they which have cast into the treasury:

For all they did cast in of their abundance: but she of her want did cast in all that she had, even all her living."

Jesus still sits by the treasury, beholding. He sees both the internal and external elements of our giving. He sees whether we give of our *"penury"* or our *"luxury"*.

He beheld *"how"* they gave; whether by sounding a trumpet before them or by not even letting the left hand know what the right hand gives. The former seeks man's approval; the latter, God's. He alone is fit to judge whether the offering is as Cain's or Abel's, who gave of the *first*-lings of his flock. (i.e., the best.) He observes whether the giver advertises his good, making sure word gets out regarding how much he gave.

Although Jesus gave particular attention to the poor widow's gift, it is fair to note that Scripture does give honorable notice of the contributions of the wealthy. However, the main point of this passage seems to relate to the widow's offering of two mites, a very insignificant amount monetarily. Yet Jesus puts this honor upon her gift, that she *"cast in more than all they which have cast into the treasury"* because she *"cast in all that she had"*. In other words, her gift counted more because it cost her more.

A little bus kid sat next to me in church one Sunday. At the offering, I dropped in my usual amount. The little girl, after watching me, opened up her little coin purse, turned it upside down and dumped all her money into the plate. (It looked like about fifty cents.) Then her face beamed into a big smile. I noticed that she seemed oblivious as to whether anyone else noticed or was impressed with her. I have the feeling that her pennies counted more than my dollars, since she gave all that she had with a cheerful heart. Mine was given without much emotion at all.

Luke 1:53
"He has filled the hungry with good things; and the rich he has sent empty away."

Although these are Mary's words rather than Jesus', we'll include them in this chapter because they are well worth our analysis.

Mary is no doubt speaking under the inspiration of the Holy Spirit according to the words of the prophet, *"your sons and daughters shall prophesy"*. (Joel 3:28)

What is this paradox which Mary utters, but very possibly does not entirely comprehend? Who are the hungry whom God fills? This may be seen in two ways: first, the hungry are those who are deprived of the pleasures and comforts of this life. They hunger for lack of even basic necessities. They wish they had a normal house or normal health, like other folks. The couple wishes they could have a child or have their child back.

A second view is that they *"hunger and thirst after righteousness"*. We have it from Jesus that these *"shall be filled"*. (Matthew 5:6) Only those who acknowledge they are lacking in righteousness shall be able to receive the righteousness of God in Christ.

However, Mary's words seem to apply more to the first view since the contrasting expression refers to the *"rich"*. So the idea is that those who have little in this life are primed to receive blessings from heavenly places. Thus, *"the poor have the gospel preached to them"*. Not all the poor receive God's *"good things"*, including the gospel. But those who hunger for them shall find no such obstacle to receiving them as did the rich young ruler who *"went away sorrowful"* and empty we might add. What are these *"good things"* God fills the hungry with?

- *"And they were all filled with the Holy Ghost."*
- *"And the disciples were filled joy and with the Holy Ghost."*
- *"You also are filled with all goodness, filled with all knowledge."*
- *"I am filled with comfort, I am exceeding joyful."*
- *"That you might be filled with all the fullness of God."*

Sounds like fun. Why would anyone want to posture himself to miss these good things by working to become rich? *"The rich he has sent away empty."* Why? They have their reward. *"But woe unto you that are rich! For you have received your consolation."* (Luke 6:24) They have comparatively little appetite or appreciation of heavenly treasure. *"Lest I be full and deny thee."* There are probably few enough rich who get *"sent away"*, since few enough seek him.

Luke 4:5-8

5. ***And the devil, taking him up into a high mountain, showed unto him all the kingdoms of the world in a moment of time.***
6. ***And the devil said unto him, all this power will I give thee, and the glory of them: for that is delivered unto me; and to whomsoever I will I give it.***
7. ***If you will therefore worship me, all shall be yours.***
8. ***And Jesus answered him and said unto him, Get thee behind me, Satan: for it is written, Thou shall worship the Lord your God, and him only shall you serve.***

Has this ever happened to you – wealth and power offered to you on a silver platter? The only catch was, you had to compromise some ethic or principle to get it. That is exactly what happened to Jesus, for he *"was in all points tempted like as we are"*. This sort of decision should not be difficult. Any Christian should be resolved to do right, no matter what the cost or consequence. There should be this sign hung at the door of our heart: NOT FOR SALE. This adage should never apply to the honesty of a believer: "Anything's for sale if the price is right".

There are those who would sin a little to gain a little, but who commend themselves that they would never sin seriously for any price. They might overestimate their mileage reimbursement, but would not think of embezzling company funds. But Jesus declined such a little temptation in refusing to turn stones into bread. Let's also remember that what seemed to be a little sin cost Adam and Eve paradise.

There are others who will maintain their integrity through the parade of little temptations, but will relent for one moment if the benefits are high enough. This is what Harry did. A pleasant man and a happily married father of five, Harry lived honestly, worked hard and loved his family. He wanted so much to provide better things for his family. One day a shady friend offered him a chance to make five thousand dollars in a single night. All Harry had to do was deliver a package to a prescribed location and accept the payment. To Harry's principled mind, it was wrong, but only a small wrong. If he didn't do it, somebody else would. Why shouldn't he get the benefit. He would do it just this once. He was right about that part. It was a set up, and he was arrested. The jury did not agree that it was a small wrong; they called it felony drug distribution. Harry served over three years in prison for it. *"Dead flies cause the ointment of the apothecary to send forth a stinking savor: so does a little folly him that is in reputation for wisdom and honor."* (Ecclesiastes 10:1) The good news is: Harry became a Christian while in prison, but it didn't have to happen that way.

The devil still says, *"All this...will I give you"*. These are powerful, tantalizing words to a man with an appetite for this world. But a good Christian will be immune to such temptations if the world is crucified unto him, and he unto the world. These sort of battles are won long before the temptation ensues. They are won by building strongholds of virtue and righteousness day after day in meditation in the Word and securing them with the mortar of prayer.

Luke 6:30&38

30. ***Give to every man that asks of you; and of him that takes away your goods ask them not again.***
38. ***Give, and it shall be given unto you; good measure, pressed down, and shaken together, and running over, shall men give into your bosom. For with the same measure that you mete withal (measure out to others) it shall be measured to you again.***

In general, Jesus is teaching us that giving should characterize the life of his disciples. We should give to *"every man"*, not just to those who will repay us or return the kindness. (See Luke 14:12) Our giving should be indiscriminate. It is very little to our credit that we give generously to our spouse or children. Do not even sinners the same? How much better when we also do kindness for inner city kids or home bound elderly.

One church bus worker noticed a gang of teenage boys in a neighborhood where he picked up kids for church every Sunday. The boys had sneered at the other kids who went to church. After praying for them for some time, the bus worker noticed that the boys had cut the top out of a five gallon bucket and taped it onto the railing of a second story staircase as a basketball goal. He walked over to the boys and addressed the oldest boy, apparently the leader. He said, "Chris, I'll make a deal with you." Chris eyed him suspiciously, "What do you mean?" The bus worker said, "I'll give you something you want if you give me something I want." Curious, Chris asked him, "Like what?" He said, "You know I've been wanting you to come visit our church for months now. So here's the deal: if you come to church with us tomorrow, I'll buy you a real basketball goal with a net and mount it right here for you." Chris accepted the deal and attended church the next day. True to his word, the bus worker bought the basketball goal and net, fabricated a mounting system to bolt it onto the same railing and came to install it. He stepped aside and taught the boys how to do all the assembly and mounting themselves. Halfway through the installation, Chris volunteered the comment, "You know what? I kinda liked your church yesterday." In time, Chris will probably turn to Christ, partly because of a few dollars strategically invested for the kingdom of God.

"Give to every man that asks of you." What we have, God may have given to us for that person's sake who will come and ask of us. Let's cast our bread upon the waters and give a portion to seven. We may thus demonstrate ourselves detached from affection toward the things of this world.

I do not think that God intends for us to do giving with receiving in mind. Yet when we do give, we have the assurance that it shall be given to us in return, and in like measure. This is not saying that the one we give to will give to us in return. Rather, Jesus is assuring us that he will personally see to it that we are recompensed. It may not come back to us in kind, and it may come to us from an entirely unexpected direction, but it will be in greater proportion to what we gave from our heart. Such a pleasant way to do business.

Luke 12:13-15

13. ***And one of the company said unto him, Master, speak to my brother, that he divide the inheritance with me.***

14. ***And he said unto him, Man, who made me a judge or a divider over you?***
15. ***And he said unto them, take heed, and beware of covetousness: for a man's life consists not in the abundance of the things which he possesses.***

The man who posed the request to Jesus seems to have a distracting preoccupation for possessions. Jesus had just expounded magnificently on the coming hazards of persecution and the wonderful enabling of the Holy Spirit in such times. We would much more have expected a comment like "*Blessed is he that shall eat bread in the kingdom of God.*" Instead, we get the impression the man wasn't paying attention to the preacher, but had his mind on money. (A common problem today.) How easily our selfish aims displace God's truths from our minds. What the man says to Jesus is the gist of too much of our praying, "God, give me money, easy money and lots of it", as if Godliness must result in gain. Jesus replies with a hint of rebuke, "*Man, who made me a judge or divider over you?*" Next Jesus gives him a double, stern warning, "*Take heed... beware.*" In clear terms, Jesus alerts the man that his soul is in danger. He is in fatal violation of the tenth commandment. We must not covet others' goods, nor set our heart so much on our own. We'd be infinitely healthier to set our affection on things above. How much better was it that Jacob desired the birthright, than that Esau desired the pottage.

Next Jesus bluntly refutes the misconception many of us hold, "*A man's life consists not in the abundance of the things which he possesses.*" This may be taken two ways: first,

Our life does not subsist by these things. That is, our sustenance is not in financial security, even if we have "*much goods laid up for many years.*" (v. 19) Though we may live long, and keep our wealth long, we may yet find ourselves unable to access it or expend it. Or we may indeed find occasion to spend our grandchildren's inheritance only to have grief or poor health render us unable to enjoy it. "*There is an evil which I have seen under the sun, and it is common among men; A man to whom God has given riches, wealth, and honor, so that he wants nothing for his soul of all that he desires, yet God gives him not power to eat thereof, but a stranger eats it*". On the other hand, we may subsist very nicely and peacefully without wealth or guaranteed income. God fed Elijah by ravens and Israel with manna, and He is pleased to supply the needs of all His own today.

Our life does not *consist* of these things. "*A man's life consists not in the abundance of the things which he possesses.*" Nor does his happiness. Rather, his life, life more abundant, eternal life, comes when the man humbles himself before God and acknowledges his need for salvation. Here is where life truly begins. All before this will seem so dead and dreary. All that follows is life indeed. Some act like their wealth and holdings will make them immortal; yet such are more likely to be the greatest hindrance to immortality. It was certainly hindering this man.

Luke 19:2,8,9

2. ***And, behold, there was a man named Zaccheus, which was the chief among the publicans, and he was rich...***
8. ***And Zaccheus stood, and said unto the Lord; Behold, Lord, the half of my goods I give to the poor; and if I have taken any thing from any man by false accusation, I restore him fourfold.***
9. ***And Jesus said unto him, This day is salvation come to this house, forasmuch as he also is a son of Abraham.***

Jesus is passing through Jericho. He will never be back. In about two weeks, He will be crucified. No one knows it but him. Zaccheus worked for the government and was very successful. Indications are that he was a good organizer and leader, because he eventually got promoted to the head of his department. However, he used his position of public trust to personal advantage. He learned how to manipulate the system to pad his own pockets.

Today, though, Zaccheus was not himself. In fact, all across Jericho something was in the air. The very breath of heaven seemed to be sweeping through town. Normally, Zaccheus was quite indifferent to the blackness of his soul. There was nothing around him to make his blackness seem black. Business owners all around him were as ruthless as he was. Even the church found ways to *"devour widows' houses"* and fleece the people in order to feather its own nest. It was a dog-eat-dog world, survival of the fittest, you know. But that day, Holiness walked into town and shook Zaccheus' value system to the core. The inner turmoil left him so restless and uneasy that he didn't even go in to work that day. He had such a fascination and fixation on Jesus that he sought to see him, to see what he was like. Maybe the divine goodness of Jesus (as Zaccheus must have heard much of) made him feel the heaviness of all his guilt, and look for some relief. As he began doing some seeking, he ran into obstacles mostly his own *short*comings. He persisted in spite of them and Jesus sort of met him half way. Something very powerful happened to Zaccheus at that point. In his heart, Zaccheus became converted (changed over) to Christ as verse six records, he *"received him joyfully."* What a contrast to the rich young ruler who also met Christ, but *"went away sorrowful."* Sometimes publicans and sinners enter the kingdom of God before the Pharisees and self-righteous. What a stunning change comes over Zaccheus! Without prompting, he stands up at dinner as if making a formal declaration, and says to Jesus, *"Behold, Lord, the half of my goods I give to the poor* (to catch up on the generosity he should have been showing all along)*; and if I have taken any thing from any man by false accusation, I restore him fourfold."* He had most certainly done so and he would probably have the records to track down all his wrongs. This was going to be very costly. It would likely cost him a big piece of the half of his wealth he did not give to the poor. Remember, he's going to repay his dishonesty four-fold. He might have to go into debt to do this. What has gotten into Zaccheus? This is about as much out of character as the Philippian Jailer hosting prisoners for dinner and preaching in his home. What got into Zaccheus was Jesus. He has been saved. *"This day is salvation come to this house."*

Notice the sequence of events:

1. Zaccheus seeks Jesus.
2. Jesus comes to Zaccheus.
3. Zaccheus receives him.
4. Zaccheus has fellowship with Jesus.
5. Zaccheus has great joy. (Probably for the first time in his life.)
6. Zaccheus acts on new found convictions, pays back old debts and shows generosity.

Can you just picture a big smile on Zaccheus' face as he makes his announcement? Maybe God gave him as much joy as he was about to give to others. The sequence of events does not necessarily work in reverse order. That is, a man does good works, finds joy and gets Jesus and eternal life as a result. No amount of good works results in eternal life. Nor is there any guarantee of joy. Joy results when good is done with a proper disposition of heart. If the purpose of the good is to make the doer happy, it's not likely to work. But if the doer's heart has been renewed by receiving Christ so that the good he does emanates from a good heart, and the intention is to make the beneficiary happy, then he himself will be profoundly happy. This kind of joy the world cannot take away. What a happy state the rich may find themselves in upon meeting Christ and discovering how much happiness their wealth can result in for others.

John 2:13-16

13. ***And the Jews' passover was at hand, and Jesus went up to Jerusalem,***
14. ***And found in the temple those that sold oxen and sheep and doves, and the changers of money sitting:***
15. ***And when he had made a scourge of small cords, he drove them all out of the temple, and the sheep, and the oxen; and poured out the changers' money and overthrew the tables;***
16. ***And said unto them that sold doves, Take these things hence; make not my Father's house a house of merchandise.***

Twice Jesus cleaned house at the temple. This is the earlier of the two incidents, which were very similar. This one happened in Jesus' first year of public ministry; the second in his final week. The second incident was discussed earlier in this chapter. (See Matthew 21:12) What he does in both incidents is virtually the same. But what he says here is significantly different than in the later incident. The objection he gives here to the Jews would apply as well today, *"Take these things hence (out); make not my Father's house a house of merchandise."* At first glance, this seems like a milder reprehension than *"you have made it a den of thieves."* Yet to simply refrain from dishonest business in the house of God, might be to allow honest trade. However, Jesus here forbids any sort of business, trade or transaction to be done in the temple. It is His Father's house. He seems to present this as a self-evident reason. Such mundane matters have no place in the house of God, where men come to meet their Maker, not a merchant; where men seek to hear what the Spirit says, not to hear the din of active commerce; where men come to *"pour out their soul before the Lord"* and to make their voice heard on high. Their ability to focus should not be hindered by distracting noise. Solomon understood this, for the temple *"was built of stone made ready before it was brought there:*

so that there was neither hammer nor axe nor any tool or iron heard in the house, while it was in building." (I Kings 6:7)

Today, our souls are the temple. When we turn our attention to seek God in prayer on our inner holy ground, let's not have our praying cluttered so much with material and monetary matters. This would be turning our prayers into a house of merchandise. Suffice it to say, *"give us this day our daily bread."* Let's be much more about the business of interceding and supplication for others, and presenting to Him our sacrifices of praise and thanksgiving. We should also keep merchandise and money out of our church buildings and our worship services as much as possible. Those who make much of money in the house of God would deserve to have God pour out their money and overthrow their tables as Jesus did.

This concludes the chapter on Jesus' teaching on wealth. Conspicuous by its absence is the fact that Jesus never taught that we should seek financial prosperity or even financial security. All his teaching inclines us to be detached from money and possessions. Such a world of snares lies in either seeking it or having it. So much wisdom and warning are in his clear, unmistakable teachings. It is alarming that they have been so misconstrued by men *"willing to justify themselves."*

"I have showed you all things, how that so laboring you ought to support the weak, and to remember the words of the Lord Jesus, how he said, It is more blessed to give than to receive."

Acts 20:35

What did the Apostles Teach About Wealth?

We find in general that both the lives and the teachings of the apostles aligned very closely with that of their Master. The apostles surely had the mind of Christ on this matter as well as all others. They also had the same Spirit that raised up Jesus from the dead dwelling in their mortal bodies, and He guided them into all truth. So it is not surprising that we find perfect congruity among them. New Testament and Old Testament speak with one voice on the subject. So do Jesus and the apostles.

Neither Jesus nor the apostles (except Judas) showed any interest in money or property. We do not find a single instance of any of them either receiving or soliciting money from anyone, whether for donation or service rendered (as Gehazi did).

Neither Jesus nor the apostles demonstrated any appetite for comforts, luxuries or the so-called "good life." There is no evidence that any of the apostles were well off financially or lived comfortably. When Peter and John went to the temple to pray, they made full financial disclosure, *"Silver and gold have I none."* Years later, when Paul was under house arrest by Governor Felix, we find that Paul had no money to offer for his own bail or release. Quite in contrast was crooked Felix, who *"hoped that money should have been given him (by) Paul, that he might loose him."* (Acts 24:26) Their choice to live modestly and simply was not so as to present such self-denial as an offering to God. It was just that their hearts were already full of a *"good matter."* They were so in love with their Lord that the things of earth grew strangely dim. They may have also decided not to encumber themselves with wealth and material possessions. Such would be a distraction and a detriment to their high calling.

Both Paul and Jesus remained financially poor by choice. Men of their caliber could have been extremely wealthy. In fact, there were times when they both had access to sizeable sums of money, but chose not to keep it. They considered themselves stewards obligated to distribute it, not consume it. In Acts 11:30, Paul and Barnabas were entrusted with a large sum of money sent to provide relief for the impoverished Christians of Judea. Paul could be safely trusted to deliver the offering because he *"coveted no man's silver, or gold, or apparel."* Jesus also was apparently given financial support to assist in the traveling expenses of the disciples. *"Judas had the bag"* it was kept in. However, in Judas' case, we're told *"he was a thief."* Both Jesus and Paul made it a practice to give to the poor, though they themselves were quite poor. In Jesus' case, it was apparently a common occurrence that he directed Judas to give their funds to someone in need. At the last supper, when Jesus sent Judas out saying, *"That you do, do quickly"*, the other apostles immediately thought that Jesus sent him *"that he should give something to the poor."* They would only think this if it happened frequently. In Paul's case, when he came to visit the church at Jerusalem, he was asked at the end of the conference to *"remember the poor."* Paul commented that was *"the same which I also was forward to do."* (Galatians 2:10)

So far were these men from being lovers of money that most of us in twenty-first century America cannot fathom such a mindset.

Now let's look to some key passages in which the apostles give us some sound doctrine on the subject of wealth. Is this God's will for us or not?

Acts 2:44 – 46

44. ***And all that believed were together, and had all things common;***

45. ***And sold their possessions and goods, and parted them to all men, as every man had need.***

46. ***And they...did eat their meat with gladness and singleness of heart...***

Soon after the early church was formed, the new Christians formed into a close-knit society. They had such love for God and each other, that each person willingly shared what they had with all the rest. This is how Jonathan loved David. This is how the husband loves his wife: all that he has, he considers to be hers. It does not appear that the apostles had commanded them to do so; they just decided spontaneously on their own. Genuine, Christ-like love cannot help but give and share. This is the sort of love for one another by which we are known to be Christ's disciples. Christ-like love does not make the goods of this world the objects of its affection. *"If any man love the world, the love of the Father is not in him."* (I John 2:15)

The sort of generosity we usually see today is nothing like what is recorded in these verses. We think of generosity as giving to our family, giving birthday gifts, sharing our home or car, or lending money to someone as long as it's repaid. However, the early Christians gave massive sums away, for they sold their possessions and goods and houses and lands, giving the proceeds to the church, as Barnabas did and as Ananias and Sapphira pretended to do. Such a consuming joy of the Lord filled them that they gave on the order of magnitude of Zaccheus, who gave half his goods to the poor and paid back four-fold on the wrongful charges he had made. But these that sowed bountifully, also reaped bountifully. Notice the harvest of happiness that resulted: *"They did eat their meat with gladness and singleness of heart.*" Please be advised that both the givers and the receivers had a nice dose of this "*gladness.*" "*It is more blessed to give than to receive.*"

There is an irony to happiness: we get more of it in giving it to others than in seeking it for ourselves.

There is an irony to happiness: we get more of it in giving it to others than in seeking it for ourselves. I would surely derive more happiness in paying several thousand dollars to get a young man in need started in college than in buying a boat and motor for fishing trips.

Someone else may deliver hot meals, at their own expense, to a homebound neighbor, in lieu of joining the bowling league. My guess is that they'd be happier with the former.

Act 8:9,18-21

9. ***But there was a certain man, called Simon, which beforetime in the same city used sorcery, and bewitched the people of Samaria, giving out that himself was some great one:***
18. ***And when Simon saw that through laying on of the apostles' hands, the Holy Ghost was given, he offered them money,***
19. ***Saying, Give me also this power, that on whomsoever I lay hands, he may receive the Holy Ghost.***
20. ***But Peter said unto him, Thy money perish with thee, because you have thought that the gift of God may be purchased with money.***
21. ***You have neither part nor lot in this matter: for your heart is not right in the sight of God.***

Here is an excerpt of one of the most remarkable stories of the power of the gospel impacting a community. Miracles of healing and regeneration worked *"great joy in that city."* Nearly the entire city of Samaria was converted under the preaching of Phillip. Peter and John were sent from Jerusalem to assist in the massive work there.

One strange character in the middle of this divine outpouring was Simon, who had been a sorcerer of great influence for a long time there. He had successfully bewitched the people with his devilish arts, yet the people mistakenly concluded, *"This man is the great power of God."* (v. 10)

We see the fundamental motive behind all of Simon's devious acts was, *"(to give) out that he was some great one."* (v. 9) This is a common practice today. Some folks will do anything to be honored and admired by others.

Even Simon though, when he saw the power of God working through the apostles, apparently repented, believed and was baptized. However, it appears that his conversion was not complete, and that he was still flawed within, as the blind man who was partially healed at first and saw men as trees walking. Simon was fascinated with Peter and John. He was amazed at how they would lay hands on the new believers and they would receive the Holy Ghost. Too much of the old self remained in Simon, for he wanted badly to have the thrill and honor of laying hands on folks to receive the Holy Ghost. He still wanted people to think he was some great one. He also still had his old values in that he offered money to Peter to give that power. What a snare it is to people who think of their money as a charm to get them anything they want. To them, money will buy them love, it will bend the law in their favor, it will appease their enemies, satisfy their own appetites, etc. *"A gift is as a precious stone in the eyes of him that has it: wherever it turns, it prospers."* (Proverbs 17:8)

Peter is not fooled by suave words, nor seduced by money; he immediately recognizes the condition of Simon's heart and soundly rebukes him, *"...your heart is not right in the sight of God...For I perceive that you are in the gall of bitterness, and in the bond of iniquity."* It is bitterness and bondage to have such an obsession as Simon did to be highly thought of.

As for the offer of money, Peter not very tactfully replied, "*Your money perish with you.*" Peter may have been offended that Simon thought him to be a man easily bribed. But Peter was doubtlessly offended at Simon disgracing the Holy Spirit and his gifts in that he "*thought that the gift of God may be purchased with money.*" Again, this dangerous thinking is rampant today. There is a tendency to think our generous offerings or gifts to the church will win us favor with God. We cheapen and insult God when we think our money will win His favor or appease His anger. Our tithes, offerings and donations are no more than gestures of obedience and expressions of gratitude.

We cheapen and insult God when we think our money will win His favor or appease His anger.

Acts 10:1-4

1. ***There was a certain man in Caesarea called Cornelius, a centurion of the band called the Italian band,***
2. ***A devout man, and one that feared God with all his house, which gave much alms to the people, and prayed to God always.***
3. ***He saw in a vision evidently about the ninth hour of the day an angel of God coming in to him, and saying, Cornelius.***
4. ***And when he looked on him, he was afraid, and said, What is it, Lord? And he said unto him, Your prayers and your alms are come up for a memorial before God.***

In the previous passage, we downplayed the role of money in our relationship with God. This passage gives a balancing perspective. "*Your prayers and your alms are come up for a memorial before God.*" God sends word to Cornelius that He's pleased with his prayers and generosity. God showed high favor to Cornelius because he exercised himself in works of faith. He did the best he could with the light he had. God would soon send someone to *"expound unto him the way of God more perfectly."* So why was Simon's offer sternly rebuked and refused, while Cornelius' alms were accepted? Because, like Abel, Cornelius' offerings were done by faith. Our good should be done with a good heart. *"For God loves a cheerful giver."*

Most of us meeting someone by the description of Cornelius would have felt sure he was a Christian and would have gladly made him a member of our church. However, the angel made it clear he was not yet saved or re-born. We halfway expect the angel to say, "Hey, nice job on your prayers and the good works thing. Keep it up and we'll see you in heaven some time." Rather, what he said was more like, "Cornelius, God knows you mean well, but without faith in the son of God, it will be impossible to please Him." The angel then directed him to go look up Peter, who just happened to be in the area and said that Peter would tell him what he ought to do. That is, how to be saved.

We must not discourage unbelievers from doing good and charitable works. Even though good works do not contribute to their salvation, they do condition him for it. Those who are inclined to good works and charitable ways are probably well disposed to hear the truth of the gospel. To such folks, let's proclaim it, as Peter did here.

Acts 20:33-35

33. *I have coveted no man's silver, or gold, or apparel.*

34. *Yea, you yourselves know, that these hands have ministered unto my necessities, and to them that were with me.*

35. *I have showed you all things, how that so laboring you ought to support the weak, and to remember the words of the Lord Jesus, how he said, It is more blessed to give than to receive.*

If any man who ever lived deserved to be free from manual, secular labor because his services were too valuable elsewhere, it was Paul. No man who ever lived was more eminently fruitful and successful in promoting and strengthening the kingdom of God. Indeed he was a *"chosen vessel."*

Consider the values and principles of this man who considered himself to be *"less than the least of all saints"*, but who was indeed *"not a whit behind the very chiefest apostles."* (II Corinthians 11:5) Maybe such a man would be worth emulating.

One of Paul's values was that he always carried his own load. *"For every man shall bear his own burden."* (Galatians 6:5) Paul had that healthy personal pride or dignity that would never let him be a free-loader. Nor would he impose himself on anyone's hospitality. He'd be much more in his own element hosting, serving, and giving to others. He strongly urged that church leaders should themselves be *"given to hospitality."* (I Timothy 3:2)

The good living we see in verses 34 and 35 are the result of the good values in verse 33. When the heart principles are right, the life will be right. He determined that he would not set his affection on unworthy objects, such as gold and apparel. Achan did, and it got him in big trouble. (Joshua 7:19-25) Paul was thus crucified to the world. It had no pull on him. Matthew Henry comments, "He could not only say with Moses & Samuel, 'Whose ox have I taken?' Or 'Whom have I defrauded?', but (Paul) could say, 'Whose kindness have I coveted, or asked?'" [6] He had come to the blessed state of not even desiring such worldly goods. What interest could money or quality clothing have for a man who had *"tasted of the heavenly gift, and (was) made partaker of the Holy Ghost?"*

Having good principles ruling in his heart, he was prepared to live right. We all need to ask, "What principles run my life?" For too many in America, the driving principle is "Get all you can." In Paul's case, it was "Give all you can." Not only would he pay his own way, but by the income derived from the work of his own hands, he would help with the necessities of those who traveled with him. Paul was skilled in the trade of tent making, and when free time permitted, he redeemed that time by working with his own hands. We should not set our hopes on getting anything free in life by such means as lottery, inheritance or handouts. It is a good principle to say, "My own hands will minister to my necessities." We will come to such a point only if we obey that command, "*Thou shalt not covet.*"

Not only did Paul contribute to the financial support of his companions, but also gave to the support of some who were weak. We ought to assist those who cannot work, not those who will not work. Keep in mind that all this giving was from his own personal wages, not from money given to him by others.

We ought to assist those who cannot work, not those who will not work.

All work is noble and good, whether a man toils and gets greasy and dirty, or whether he exercises only his intellect. Let neither disparage the other, and let not those who do not work or do not have to work think poorly of those who do.

Paul powerfully reinforces his case by quoting the very words of Jesus, "*It is more blessed to give than to receive.*" Let's align ourselves with Paul and Jesus and the more excellent segment of our race who find more enjoyment in helping than having.

Romans 12:8

8. ***He that gives, let him do it with simplicity.***

Those who are loathe to depart with their money or goods are prone to make some fanfare about giving it away. But Jesus urges us, *"Do not sound a trumpet before you, as the hypocrites do in the synagogues and in the streets."* How much better to give anonymously or to make very little of it. It detracts a great deal from the gift when the donor regularly makes mention of it to acquaintances and often thereafter reminds the recipient. It is far more gracious to *"Let another man praise you and not your own mouth."* (Proverbs 27:2) When a gift is given or an alms is performed, it would be in keeping with the spirit of these scriptures to:

a. Avoid any future discussion of your alms. Try either changing the subject or reminding the receiver of like kindnesses they have done.
b. Downplay the value of the gift or kindness done. "Well I don't know what I'd have used it for."
c. Never mention it to anyone else. *"Let not your left hand know what your right hand is doing."* (Or has done.)
d. Do the giving privately, rather than publicly. This could be very embarrassing for the receiver.
e. Do the kindness and leave promptly, without waiting for a "thank you" or even an acknowledgement.
f. Have someone else make the delivery, like a child.
g. Never insinuate that you expect something in return.

Galatians 6:7,8

7. ***Be not deceived; God is not mocked: for whatsoever a man sows, that shall he also reap.***
8. ***For he that sows to his flesh shall of the flesh reap corruption; but he that sows to the Spirit shall of the spirit reap life everlasting.***

The preamble to this verse gives notice that what follows is hard to believe or accept. So many think that they can live as they please and escape the moral and natural consequences. Judgment and punishment are for bad people, not me. But the Scripture warns, *"Be not deceived."* We have the mistaken impression that we may somehow dodge or evade the approaching consequences of our actions. We figure we'll beat the odds. But again, the Bible gives stern admonition, *"Be sure your sin will find you out."* (Numbers 32:23) God will see to it. He is not mocked or fooled. Our limited success with man in dodging the law, sweet-talking and lying our way out of trouble makes us cocky and self-assured. We think the same tactics will work with God. Never happen. We can pay now or we can pay later, but we will pay for our actions.

However, this verse is also an encouragement to do good. We are just as surely to have recompense for our kindness as the sinner is to get retribution. Let us fear God for these things, for He is almighty, sovereign and just.

"Whatsoever a man sows." There is a collective effect of the life we live. All our actions and interactions work toward a composite result, which is what we sow for the future. We may have a lifestyle of giving or of greed. Whether we realize it or not, we are continually sowing good seed or bad seed.

"That shall he also reap." If we cast our bread upon the waters, it shall come back to us after many days. Or if we bilk what we can out of anyone we can, we shall receive the wages of it just as surely. "But I'll never see that person again; what does it matter how I treat him?" Or, "If I be good to the people I expect to be around in the future and gouge the folks I'll never see again, I'll have good times to look forward to, right? I've beaten the system." Wrong. The problem is: there is a God, and He judges righteously. *"That shall he also reap"* is not saying that how we treat others is how they will treat us. Rather it asserts that how we treat others is how *God* will treat us. He will see to it that we receive precisely the crop of treatment that corresponds to the seed we planted.

"He that sows to his flesh shall of the flesh reap corruption." Sooner or later our bodies will die and corrupt. All the pleasures, cares, nurture, exercise, feeding, gratification and pampering we invest in our own body all comes to nothing in the end. If we indulge ourselves with sinful greed and excess of pleasures, it corrupts both body and soul. If we feed the flesh nature in us the *"lust of the flesh, and the lust of the eyes, and the pride of life,"* we will reap this *"corruption"* as our reward. As Jeremiah's linen girdle corrupted when he buried it in the earth, so when we put all that we are into this earth and do not invest in heaven, we become corrupted, *"marred"* and *"profitable for nothing."* (Jeremiah 13:1-7)

"He that sows to the Spirit shall of the Spirit reap life everlasting." The one who sows to the flesh simply receives the natural consequence of his actions. But he who sows spiritual good is not recompensed by only natural responses; he is rewarded *"of the Spirit."* That is, God, the Holy Spirit, ensures that we reap the good results of our good living. The world system cannot reward a man for living by faith, waiting on God, being constant in prayer, or for being *"steadfast, immovable, always abounding in the work of the Lord."* Nothing on earth can forgive sins, make us adopted sons or award us eternal life. This has to be given *"of the Spirit"*, or by the Spirit. The Scripture most emphatically declares, *"your labor is not in vain in the Lord."* (I Corinthians 15:58)

What is sowing to the Spirit? It is doing those works or acquiring those dispositions that tend to the increase of the Spirit of Christ in us. Setting our minds to love God with all the mind and heart, and improving in our love of our neighbor would

Sowing to the Spirit is doing those works or acquiring those dispositions that tend to the increase of the Spirit of Christ in us.

be sowing to the Spirit. Where we sow our treasure is where we must expect to reap. There are really only three places where we sow treasure: to God, to neighbor, and to self. All that we have in banks, equities, stocks and properties is really sowing to self. Remember: all that goes to corruption. All that we give to our church or Christian ministries is giving to God. Similarly, all charitable giving to people would also be giving to God. Giving to God and neighbor would be sowing to the Spirit, if done in the proper motive.

Ephesians 1:3,11,13,14

3. ***Blessed be the God and Father of our Lord Jesus Christ, who has blessed us with all spiritual blessings in heavenly places in Christ:***
11. ***In whom also we have obtained an inheritance, being predestinated according to the purpose of him who works all things after the counsel of his own will:***
13. ***In whom you also trusted, after that you heard the word of truth, the gospel of your salvation: in whom also after that you believed, you were sealed with that holy Spirit of promise,***
14. ***Which is the earnest of our inheritance until the redemption of the purchased possession, unto the praise of his glory.***

Upon reading this text, I can see where someone would think, "What could this possibly teach us about money or wealth? It isn't even mentioned." That is exactly the point. In verse three, Paul begins to speak the high praises of God. Then he magnificently enumerates all the glorious blessings he imparts to those who are "*in Christ*", that is, to those who have invited him into their hearts and have been born again. To such folk apply all the indescribable honors and blessings which follow. The source of it all is *"heavenly places."* Consequently, we may expect them to be divine and truly excellent in nature. We are told:

a. He has made us to be holy and without blame! It is hard to imagine a greater gift than the dismissing of all charges of sin against us and the declaring of us to be legally righteous.
b. v.5 We have been adopted as children of the Highest. How could any higher honor be bestowed on someone?
c. v.6 We have been made acceptable to God *"in the beloved."* This is particularly remarkable since we *"were sometime alienated and enemies in (our) mind by wicked works, yet now has he reconciled."*
d. v.7 We are redeemed out of the realm of darkness, the price of which was the very blood of Christ. No greater service or sacrifice has ever been done for any man!
e. v.9 As to a very close and beloved friend, he has revealed the previously unknown mysteries of his will, *"which things the angels desired to look into"* and of which *"prophets have enquired and searched diligently."* (I Peter 1:12,10)
f. v.10 We obtain an inheritance. We are heirs of God and heirs of his kingdom. Such grace has God shown to us!
g. v.13,14 As if the foregoing were not already infinitely above all that we could ask or think, we are also *"sealed with the Holy Spirit of promise, which is the earnest of our inheritance."* God imparts to us the very essence of the Holy Spirit. God lives within us! Peter calls this an *"exceeding great and precious promise: that ...you might be partakers of the divine nature."* Absolutely astounding!

Now imagine how utterly out of place it would be to say, "Oh, he also gives us money."

If we place higher regard and greater attention to material wealth than these real blessings from heavenly places, then we make ourselves to be as carnal as Esau who foolishly gave up his birthright for a meal of pottage. Esau's reasoning was, *"What profit shall this birthright do to me?"* Let us not be so shallow and ignorant of these things, since we have revealed to us so much of the canon of Scripture. Let us value our spiritual birthright *now,* remembering that later when Esau finally realized his great loss, he could not get it back, *"though he sought it carefully with tears."*

Ephesians 3:16-19

16. ***That he would grant you, according to the riches of his glory, to be strengthened with might by his Spirit in the inner man;***

17. ***That Christ may dwell in your hearts by faith; that you, being rooted and grounded in love,***

18. ***May be able to comprehend with all saints what is the breadth, and length, and depth, and height;***

19. ***And to know the love of Christ, which passes knowledge, that you might be filled with all the fullness of God.***

This is Paul, giving the sum and substance of his praying for the Ephesian Christians. No father ever desired more to see his children do well and prosper than Paul did for the Ephesians, and the Colossians, the Boreans, the Philippians, etc. I imagine he spent more time in prayer than in any other activity from day to day. These four verses match closely to some of his other prayers recorded in scripture. Notice that conspicuous by its absence is the mention of any material or monetary gain. Nowhere in the Bible do we see Paul praying for himself or anyone else to acquire worldly gain. To wise, fatherly Paul, such things were irrelevant to their well-being. He likely considered wealth to be more hazardous than helpful. Jesus probably had wealth and prosperity in mind when he prayed, "lead them not into temptation."

Nowhere in the Bible do we see Paul praying for himself or anyone else to acquire worldly gain.

In *not* praying for riches, Paul showed that he had a very low regard for them. Such people may be trusted as stewards of it. When Solomon prayed only for wisdom, God gave him wisdom *and* riches and honor.

Ephesians 5:5

5. ***For this you know, that no whoremonger, nor unclean person, nor covetous man, who is an idolater, has any inheritance in the kingdom of Christ and of God.***

This is powerful language, soundly condemning what is apparently very serious and fatal sins. That the three sins mentioned were dangerous enough to exclude someone from the kingdom of God was common knowledge in the early church: "*for this you know.*" Even in the first century, whoremongers were widely condemned. If they had been asked, they would likely have said they were not going to heaven. Such flagrant and immoral conduct left no room for denial. Likewise with the unclean person: his filthy words, thoughts and vile acts gave him such a sense of corruption, that he could hardly imagine himself going to heaven. But the covetous man typically has no such sense of personal ruin. Usually, all the ways of a covetous man are clean in his own eyes. He would not agree that he is covetous, or that coveting is such a big deal. "I didn't steal anything, did I? What's the harm of just wishing I had it?" The covetous man would be very offended to be put in association with such shameful characters as a whoremonger and an unclean person. Yet the verse singles out the coveter and adds to his guilt in saying that he is an idolater. And the conviction expressed at the end of the verse appears to target the covetous man maybe even more than the others, "*has any inheritance in the kingdom of Christ and of God.*" It's as if the Holy Spirit is saying, "If your heart is set so much on the things of this world, you have no heart for and no treasure in the kingdom of heaven."

If your heart is set so much on the things of this world, you have no heart for and no treasure in the kingdom of heaven.

Philippians 3:7

7. ***But what things were gain to me, those I counted loss for Christ.***

This statement very well applies to many "prospering" Christians today. All the assets, properties, goods and investments they have gained amount to a corresponding loss of heart, time and labor for God. It is next to impossible to have much and keep from thinking often and fondly of it. The heart tends to continually ponder these things. Mary pondered better things in her heart. The only escape from such obsessive preoccupation of one's wealth is the counsel Jesus gave one such rich man, *"If you wish to be perfect, go and sell that you have, and give to the poor, and you shall have treasure in heaven: and come and follow me."* Then it may be said, "What things were loss to me, are now gain for Christ." Why? Because the man is now wonderfully freed from the cares of this world and the deceitful of riches and is able to love and serve God more fully.

Philippians 4:15-19

15. ***Now you Philippians know also, that in the beginning of the gospel, when I departed from Macedonia, no church communicated with me as concerning giving and receiving, but you only.***
16. ***For even in Thessalonica you sent once and again unto my necessity.***

17. ***Not because I desire a gift: but I desire fruit that may abound to your account.***
18. ***But I have all, and abound: I am full, Having received of Epaphroditus the things which were sent from you, an odor of a sweet smell, a sacrifice acceptable, well pleasing to God.***
19. ***But my God shall supply all your need according to his riches in glory by Christ Jesus.***

The church at Philippi in Greece (Macedonia) was one of the more faithful churches. The reason could be that they saw Paul (and Silas) suffer for righteousness' sake. Remember, that was where they were arrested on false charges, illegally beaten and imprisoned. Here, Paul commends this church for financially supporting Paul and Silas as they preached. Very likely, nearly every church Paul helped plant supported him while he was with them, but the Philippians distinguished themselves in continuing to support Paul even after he left the area. When Paul had moved on to a neighboring city, Thessalonica, and began preaching there, the Philippians continued their support, *"once and again."* These later offerings sent to Paul were very different from the times they supported Paul when he was among them. When he was with them, their financial support was fair exchange for Paul's services in preaching to them and pastoring them. This corresponds to the salaries we pay the pastors of our churches. When Paul left and began preaching and serving elsewhere, then the Philippians' support of Paul did not result in any service to themselves. This was evidence of much greater love, much greater generosity and much more loyalty to Christ and his gospel. This kind of giving corresponds to our support of missions around the world. This kind of selfless, unrequited giving moved Paul, in the Spirit, to write, *"My God shall supply all your need according to his riches in glory by Christ Jesus."* (v. 19) This wonderful assurance is for the Philippians, and any other believers who likewise give sacrificially to the gospel.

Because their giving is bestowed somewhere that is highly unlikely to reciprocate, God himself does the rewarding. *"And you shall be blessed; for they cannot recompense you; for you shall be recompensed at the resurrection of the just."* (Luke 14:14)

Philippians 4:19 is one of the most often quoted verses in the Bible. It is also one of the most misapplied. Many of us have tried to give scriptural encouragement to someone going through financial hardships. We point them to this verse and say, "See? God promises to supply all your needs." However, the promise applies only to obedient, gospel supporting Christians. If we want to use the verse to encourage our friend, we must present the responsibility along with the privilege. We could say, "Jim, would you like God to supply all your needs especially in times like this? Then do your duty in supporting your church and the gospel."

Finally, let's remember that the promise is that we would receive according to *"his riches in glory,"* not just our carnal needs or daily bread. Let us look expectantly for those heavenly riches as well.

Colossians 3:2

Set your affections on things above, not on things on the earth.

Every command in the Bible, such as the one here, implies an ability to perform. We are commanded, for our good, to *"set (our) affections on things above,"* therefore we are able to do so. We may bridle and steer our affections anywhere we please. If we are not careful in this, we could end up loving the most unworthy of objects, such as a bass boat, the internet, or another man's property. We must guard very carefully the things we allow ourselves to love. The NIV gives Proverbs 4:23 this way, *"Above all else, guard your heart, for it is the wellspring of life."* No one will be exonerated at judgment with an excuse like, "But I couldn't help it; I fell in love with them." "Well I just love fishing" is a lousy excuse for neglecting children who need a Daddy. We are to *set* our affection, *set* our heart on the proper things to love. Among those things is setting our love on things above; that is, our heavenly Father, our soon to be heavenly home, the gospel of Christ, which is from above, the church of God, which is soon to be above. We should love the things, and value the things that God does. He values the soul of a man above all the wealth of the material world. (Mark 8:36) So should we. He values the cultivating of a child's sanctification above the child's education. So should we. God desires more to see our children fitted for and acquainted with things of heaven, than to be wise to the world. So should we.

Likelier than not, our affections, un-harnessed, would gravitate toward cheaper, carnal interests. For most of us, who have our affections misplaced to begin with, we have need to re-set our affections to things above, maybe daily.

Colossians 3:23,24

23. ***And whatsoever you do, do it heartily, as to the Lord, and not unto men.***
24. ***Knowing that of the Lord you shall receive the reward of the inheritance; for you serve the Lord Christ.***

It is too often the case that wages are not equivalent to the service or labor provided. It is not very often that God's children get proper credit from employers or other folks they have done good for. The scripture says never mind the lack of acknowledgement or recognition. God sees it. Wherever man fails to adequately compensate, God will supply more than adequately. Whatever we sow, we reap, whether man rewards us or not. Knowing this, we may do our labor or our good heartily, for "*of the Lord (we) shall receive the reward.*" Since God observes all work that we do, and since everything the Christian does reflects on the Lord, we do indeed "*serve the Lord Christ.*" He considers it to be so. Thus, he will pay our wages when no one else does. What a privilege to be a servant of the living God.

Colossians 4:1

Masters, give unto your servants that which is just and equal, knowing that you also have a Master in heaven.

"Masters" would include company owners, managers or anyone in a position to decide on employees' pay. There are two approaches to setting pay rates. First, get the best skilled employee and get the maximum production out of him for the minimum investment of pay. This is the usual approach by people in business for the money, who don't care who they have to step on to get it. *"He that makes haste to be rich shall not be innocent."* (Proverbs 28:20) The second is: get skilled employees and pay them a fair wage (or better), a wage commensurate with their service. God would be displeased with a man who exploits his employees to maximize his own profits. Every employee ought to give his best effort and every employer ought to give his best wage.

I Thessalonians 5:14

Now we exhort you, brethren…support the weak…

This is an obligation to every one of us, Christian or not. Every society and culture has its strong and capable as well as its weak. The strong and wise are well able to provide for their own necessities and usually far above their own needs. However, we must never think that we may keep all that we earn. Besides legitimate obligations such as taxes and tithes, and proper support of our own wives and children, God also tasks us with caring for the weak around us.

Well who are the *"weak?"* Who is our neighbor? Whoever needs our help, as the one who fell among thieves. Some of us have relatives who are unable to hold a job that pays adequately. We are to supply their lack. Others cannot handle any more than simple cleaning jobs. They could not subsist on their own, much less than support children besides. It wouldn't hurt for a company to keep such a person on the payroll anyway. They can be taught to do simple things that may not even be worth minimum pay. Keeping them would be a huge kindness to them, though a slight burden to the company. In this way, the owner is supporting the weak in a way that wonderfully elevates their sense of self-worth. God would bless such a company more than the owner would imagine.

Who are the "*weak?*" Our very old and our very young. They are our sick and our handicapped folks. They are the emotionally distraught or bereaved. These are temporarily weak and will likely recover in time. But while they are hurting, how blessed it would be if the boss said, "I know this is a very hard time for you. I'm giving you two weeks off – full pay. Let me know if you need more time." God will surely repay this boss. Just as likely, the person he did it for will probably become one of his most loyal, hardest working employees, many times over repaying him for the kindness.

I Timothy 4:1

Now the Spirit speaks expressly that, in the latter times, some shall depart from the faith, giving heed to seducing spirits, and doctrines of devils.

"*The Spirit speaks expressly*", but we hear darkly or vaguely. Yet here the warning is clear: it shall be a sign of the end times that, maybe more than usual, there shall be seducing spirits working in men, some of whom speak unwittingly the doctrine of devils. Paul later prophesies that "*evil men and seducers shall (become) worse* and *worse.*" (II Timothy 3:13) Thus as the end approaches and the rapture of the saints and the return of Christ become imminent, we may expect false doctrine and seductive men to rise to such a crescendo of deceit and credibility, that if it were possible they could deceive the very elect. The very worst and last of seducers will be the antichrist himself. But in the times just preceding him, we will likely see some of the most believable, seeming religious preachers declaring things that must be very amiable to carnal minds. The seductive element implies a pleasant, though false message. It also implies intent to draw away from truth.

"Doctrines of devils" is not what we would normally think. We would expect the enemy to come moving many to devil worship, drug abuse, murder or tampering with the occult. We think of seducers as David Koresh of the Branch Davidians or the Jim Jones cult in which 400 or so followers died drinking a deadly potion. However, far greater damage is done in other false doctrines which seem good and consequently, are able to seduce many more into error. This makes it all the more devilish. Remember, *"the serpent was more subtle than any beast of the field which the Lord God had made."* (Genesis 3:1) Any fisherman knows that the best lures are the ones that most closely approximate a real fish. Likewise the devil knows that his most effective lures are those that most closely resemble the truth. Satan even uses scripture to deceive. *"If you be the Son of God, cast yourself down; for it is written, He shall give his angels charge concerning you, and in their hands they shall bear you up, lest at any time you dash your foot against a stone."* (Matthew 4:6)

In I Timothy 4:1, two problems are at work simultaneously. First, some professed believers will depart from their faith. Second, seducing spirits will be rampant, targeting victims who are vulnerable to false doctrine. The picture is sheep on the outskirts of the flock straying carelessly too far from the voice of the Shepherd. Such are particularly susceptible to *"seducing spirits."* Our greatest defense against error is truth – God's truth, the Bible. Yet so many do not read or do not heed its words. It alarms me how many Christians have never read the Bible through even once. More disturbing are the numbers of teachers and even preachers who have never read the Bible completely through! Failure to know the word of God leaves us gullible toward any doctrine that seems nice at face value.

To put it very plainly, the doctrine of health and wealth has Satan's fingerprints all over it.

To put it very plainly, the doctrine of health and wealth has Satan's fingerprints all over it. It certainly tastes good to the soul, it is pleasant to the eyes and has promise of making men wise. The message comes to us with such subtlety that we hear it in the house of God from the preacher. Even passages from the Bible are used in an attempt to support the doctrine. However, just as Satan misused a passage to tempt Christ, so it is done today to tempt us. We must be sharply wary of a speaker reading things into scripture that are not there. We must also be familiar enough with the Bible as a whole to know when someone is taking a statement out of context and interpreting it in a way that contradicts so many other clear mandates of scripture. The idea that "God wants me to have the best" (meaning I can live wealthily and have everything I want in this life) cannot be reconciled with "*lay not up for yourselves treasures upon earth*" and "*if any man will come after me, let him deny himself*" and "*take heed, and beware of covetousness; for a man's life consists not in the abundance of the things which he possesses.*" It is a doctrine of devils that God wants us to be rich materially. Granted, the doctrine is spoken mostly by honest, well-meaning men of God, but their words promote worldliness, rather than a proper affection for heaven. Satan would love nothing more than to divert Christian's affections away from heavenly treasure and to this world. He would love nothing more than to see prosperous Christians gratify themselves with all their wealth, rather than supporting the spread of the gospel or providing relief for the hurting.

There are a lot of seducing spirits today – more than ever. But the seducing spirit behind the false doctrine of health and wealth is one of the clearest fulfillments of this prophecy today. Jesus warned, *"Many false prophets shall rise, and shall deceive many."* Peter warned, *"Save yourselves from this (crooked) generation."* (Acts 2:40)

I Timothy 6:17-19

17. ***Charge them that are rich in this world, that they be not high-minded, nor trust in uncertain riches but in the living God, who gives us richly all things to enjoy;***
18. ***That they do good, that they be rich in good works, ready to distribute, willing to communicate (share).***
19. ***Laying up in store for themselves a good foundation against the time to come, that they may lay hold on eternal life.***

The word of God here does not condemn anyone for being rich, but it does give them a string of cautions and instructions. These are well worth noting.

The first warning is ***"that they be not high-minded."*** It is a very natural tendency for those who are very successful in this life to think very highly of themselves or to become arrogant. Yet if they become wealthy at the cost of becoming arrogant, they have lost out. They will need the grace of God to resist or reverse this besetting pride. How pleasant is the rare exception who can handle success and wealth and yet retain such graces as humility and kindness.

The second warning is not to ***"trust in uncertain riches."*** Here is a snare that is all but inescapable. With man, this is impossible; but with God all things are possible. There is a deceitfulness in riches that promises occasion to eat, drink and be merry for a long time to come. But riches are uncertain. *All* riches are uncertain, especially in a sue-happy society. Even if riches could be certain for this life, they can avail nothing in the next. *"For we brought nothing into this world, and it is certain we can carry nothing out."* (I Timothy 6:7)

Next, we're told what *is* certain and what we are to trust in: ***"the living God."*** He alone is steadfast, solid and unfailingly reliable. Even the best of men and institutions are but sinking sand by comparison. No one who trusts in him and evidences that trust by obedience will be disappointed in him. One good reason why we should trust him is that he ***"gives us richly all things to enjoy."*** Why shouldn't we trust in the Divine Father who so loves the world and has such benevolent thoughts toward us continually?

In addition to the warnings, rich folk are given instructions. First, ***"that they do good."*** Of course, we are all to do good, but the rich are in a particularly advantageous position to do so. They have more wealth with which to do good, and in some cases, the wealth gives them more liberty to devote themselves to God's service as well. In other cases, the wealth can be enslaving.

To whom are they to do good? They are to *"do good unto all men, especially unto them who are of the household of faith."* (Galatians 6:10) We should do good as opportunity arises as when the good Samaritan came across the wounded man. We can figure that when we come across a need that no one else is aware of or has ability to supply the need, God must have meant for us to handle it.

One church bus driver, upon dropping off the last two children, got off the bus and talked with the father. The bus driver asked if there was anything he could do for the family. The father scratched his head a moment and then mentioned that his five year old daughter, Samantha, had a badly decayed tooth which needed extracting. The tooth had blackened and that became Samantha's nickname at school – Black Tooth. A dentist had told him it would cost $165.00 to remove it. The father was struggling to scrape the money together, so he asked if the church could help. That night, a special collection was taken at the church amounting to $227.00. The money was delivered to the family that night. They were told they could keep the change. A couple of days later, a local dentist removed the tooth with no complications. When he heard that a church had donated money to pay for it, he reduced his fee to $60.00. The father was speechless with gratitude.

On another occasion, the Highland Baptist Church of Pass Christian, Mississippi, had struggled for twelve years with a five hundred dollar per month building note. It was a small country church, consisting of working class families. When I became pastor in 1995, I challenged the church to pay off the remaining $23,500.00 by the end of 1996. The members gasped at the thought of attempting such a feat. (The church's annual income was averaging $35,000.00.) However, after a valiant effort by the church, we came within $4000.00 of our goal a week before Christmas. That Sunday morning, a well-to-do woman approached me just before the morning service. She asked, "How much does the church still owe on its note?" I told her, "Right at $4000.00." She sat down, wrote a check out for that amount and handed it to me saying, "Well now it's paid for." (I started to tell her I only owed $40,000.00 on my house note, but I refrained.) Moments later, I announced to the congregation that a donor, who wished to remain anonymous, just completed paying off the church note. The woman who gave the check sat incognito in the middle of the church as an enthusiastic cheer erupted. She smiled peacefully. I have to think that the memory of that day and that gift will linger pleasantly in her mind the rest of her life. What pleasant memories do you have?

Our verse goes on: the rich are to be ***"rich in good works."*** They are able to do so, and therefore they should. *"Rich"* here could mean plentiful or it could refer to magnitude. After a terrible hurricane ravaged Honduras, a group of south Mississippi medical doctors teamed up to first build and then voluntarily staff a charity-type hospital in that country. This was all done with their personal finances and time. That's being rich in good works. Barnabas sold his land and gave all the proceeds to the apostles. This likely helped many fledgling new believers to tarry in Jerusalem to be discipled. Who can calculate the magnitude of benefit which resulted from these two cases?

Recently, I had occasion to watch the annual Gulf Coast Sailing Championships. I was invited to watch the races on a forty eight foot luxury yacht. The host could not have been kinder and the outing could not have been more enjoyable. The boat valued at about $300,000.00 to $400,000.00. The owner probably uses the boat four to six times per year. I could not help but think how much good that much money could do in the support of overseas missions or in helping growing churches fulfill their potential. Am I just spoiling somebody's fun? Not at all. The very verse we're analyzing says that God *"gives us richly all things to enjoy."* But those who choose not to spend it all on themselves, but rather give also to worthy causes, will surely have greater internal peace, real happiness and satisfaction. It is important to remember that rich giving does not result in salvation; rather salvation should result in such rich giving. When true believers give themselves and their possessions to needs around them, that is ***"laying up in store for themselves a good foundation against the time to come"*** though they may deplete their stores in this life.

Rich giving does not result in salvation; rather salvation should result in such rich giving.

The believing rich man is to be rich in good works and ***"ready to distribute."*** This is having a heart to give away what is rightfully his. The next phrase, ***"willing to communicate (share)"*** would relate more to what a man keeps as his own property, but is willing and happy to share. This would be like the man who took a number of us for a ride on his luxury yacht. It is a little more justifiable to have and keep much if we share much.

II Timothy 2:4

No man that wars entangles himself with the affairs of this life, that he may please him who has chosen him to be a soldier.

Imagine how ludicrous this would be. Two combat marines are advancing on a sniper position. One says to his buddy, "Cover me while I charge him and we'll capture him." His buddy says, "You bet," and aims toward the sniper, waiting for him to show himself. As the first man makes the charge, the cover man gets a call on his cell phone. He answers it and discusses with his real estate agent a possible sale of some property. Toward the end of the phone call, someone taps him on the shoulder. It's his partner, all shot up and bloodied, uniform tattered, and with a rather annoyed expression on his face. "Sorry to interrupt you, but I thought you were going to cover me." What a lousy soldier! But this is where too many American believers are: trying to serve both God and money. Money matters so infest our minds, it's a wonder we can focus on anything else. Preoccupation with the cares of this life hampers us from serving God with all our mind, soul and strength.

I don't believe we can make a one time decision to follow Christ and serve him rather than our own selfish gain. We must crucify selfish desire daily. This desire, like stubborn weeds, needs to be cut back daily. Paul said, *"I die daily."* Jesus said we must deny ourselves and take up our cross *daily* and follow him. We have to decide every day whether we're going to please God above all else.

Titus 1:10, 11

10. ***For there are many unruly and vain talkers and deceivers, specially they of the circumcision,***

11. *Whose mouths must be stopped, who subvert whole houses, teaching things which they ought not, for filthy lucre's sake.*

Men using a pretense of religion to bilk money out of unsuspecting followers is nothing new. Paul is here warning Titus of the same thing. Not only do they successfully get their hands on other peoples' money, but they also inject dangerous false doctrines into their minds. These false teachers do not speak things which are becoming to sound doctrine, but rather their talk is "*vain*", that is, useless in instructing to do righteousness. They are "*unruly*" because they refuse to be ruled or governed. They rebel against truth in the Bible and will not stand to be corrected. The Bible is not open for any private interpretation. It means what it says. Such false teachers are very dangerous. They are said to "*subvert*" whole households. The Greek word translated here as "*subvert*", is *anatrepho*. This is the only occurrence of this word in the Bible and it is a very strong expression meaning "to ruin or completely destroy." Wrong doctrine can be fatal to a man's soul. We used to say in the Navy, "You can die on bum gouge (bad information)." Peter calls such wrong doctrine or teaching of such false teachers "*damnable heresies*", meaning they can result in the damning of souls. (II Peter 2:1) We must not take lightly differences in doctrines and beliefs. Buying into false doctrine can have disastrous effects in this life and the next. We must not be so foolish as Gallio who relegated religious controversies to being no more than "*a question of words and names, and of your law*", for "*Gallio cared for none of those things.*" (Acts 18:15,17)

Because of the extensive damage that can be done by false doctrine and twisting of scripture, the Holy Spirit presses upon us with urgency that their mouths must be stopped. This is accomplished not by persecutions and executions, but by sound doctrine and Biblical preaching. (Titus 1:9) We can be effective in contending for the faith only by becoming an expert in the Bible.

Last, we see the underlying and hidden motive of false teachers: "*for filthy lucre's sake.*" Religious phonies and their false doctrine are some of those evils that find their root in the love of money. See what a death grip the love of money can get on a man, that he would toy with the eternal life of others to achieve his ends. Two major symptoms of false religious teachers are an obsession for power and for money. They commonly isolate their potential followers from other religious leaders. This cuts off a source of rescue. The usual strategy is that they will gradually exert more and more control (power) over their followers, eventually getting more and more into their finances. They must do their deeds in the dark, because they will not hold up to the light of scriptural scrutiny.

Hebrews 10:34

For you had compassion on me in my bonds, and took joyfully the spoiling of your goods, knowing in yourselves that you have in heaven a better and an enduring substance.

Although the book of Hebrews is unsigned, this verse gives some indication that Paul may be the writer of it, though the Holy Spirit is the true author. Paul spent several years in prison, from where he wrote many of the New Testament books.

Notice the indication of persecution of his day: imprisonment (and sometimes execution) of Christian leaders. Paul, Peter, John, Stephen, James, Sosthenes, Silas and others were all arrested. Some were beaten, some were killed, others left in prison a long time. Another probably more widespread form of persecution was the seizing, or spoiling, of Christians' property. What is the Christian's response? Retaliation or revenge? Such tactics only perpetuate hostilities and hint that the Christian must have loved his possessions. Rather, the Hebrew Christians were proper in enduring "*joyfully the spoiling of (their) goods.*" Yet they were not being foolish, or pretending to be joyful in order to minimize the pleasure of the evildoers. They were genuinely joyful. There were several reasons for this:

a. **They did not love much their things in this world.** Although the early Christians were taught to avoid developing affection for inanimate possessions, their detachment from such probably stemmed more from being filled with the spirit of Christ and having much love for him. Maybe you've noticed that when a person is enough in love with someone, material wealth shrinks in significance. Normally, losing one's possessions would be cause for grief, but they did not grieve for what they did not love.
b. **They believed the word of Christ.** Jesus had taught the people, *"Blessed are you when men shall… persecute you for my sake."* They knew that they stood to be greatly blessed as a result. The apostles understood this when they were beaten in the presence of the council, yet they departed *"rejoicing that they were counted worthy to suffer shame for his name."* The early Christians counted it an honor to suffer for the name of Christ and they had frequent occasion to do so.
c. **They believed in heavenly reward.** Jesus had taught them that they would receive a hundredfold now in this time and in the world to come, eternal life. *"Rejoice…for great is your reward in heaven."* Faith gives victory over any such adversity. They willingly, or rather gladly, forfeited their belongings on earth, which are uncertain and so easily evaporate, in order to obtain a more excellent reward, *"a better and an enduring substance."*

Could we of twenty-first century America attain to the same mindset? With our stock market, IRA's, six digit household incomes and with more money on our person than the average family outside the U.S. will make in a month? Yes, we can do it, by the grace of God.

And we can develop a healthy detachment from the love of money more easily than the Hebrew Christians did, who suffered the violent, unjust confiscation of their property. We may follow the same prescription Jesus gave another rich man, "*Go and sell what you have, and give to the poor, and you shall have treasure in heaven.*" And if your treasure is there, guess where your heart will be?

We have such unprecedented opportunity today. We may see live footage of the needs and opportunity for the gospel all over the world. We see this, not in the frustration of just *wishing* we could do something, but rather most of us have the financial means to really help. Americans today have more negotiable income than any people group in history. Some of you may be thinking, "Sure, I've got negotiable income; I can pay the car note or I can pay my medical bills this month." It is true that too many of us have spent and borrowed to the hilt. But with a little bit of financial discipline, we can get our spending considerably below our income. Then we can collectively make a massive impact in the world in financing the Great Commission. But it all begins with loving God above all else and our neighbor as ourselves.

Hebrews 11:24-27

24. ***By faith Moses, when he was come to years, refused to be called the son of Pharaoh's daughter,***

25. ***Choosing rather to suffer affliction with the people of God than to enjoy the pleasures of sin for a season,***

26. ***Esteeming the reproach of Christ greater riches than the treasures in Egypt; for he had respect unto the recompense of the reward.***

27. ***By faith he forsook Egypt, not fearing the wrath of the king; for he endured, as seeing him who is invisible.***

This is what I love about the Old Testament: it is full of vivid, real life illustrations of Bible truths. The message here is that Moses declined great wealth, ease and power, preferring to seek a greater, higher and more lasting reward. So many in America put all their strength and years into gaining wealth. Yet Moses had it to begin with and decided it wasn't worth it. He made this decision *before* he met God and heard his voice. How much more must he have disdained the best this world had to offer *after* he encountered the God of Abraham, Isaac and Jacob; and saw the glory of God in defeating his enemies and providing a table in the wilderness for an entire nation. Moses found a more excellent joy in serving our righteous God and in serving his generation. He had already tried the life of luxury, ease, wealth and power. He must have found it to be very dull and hollow. Too much of such a life can be very boring and empty. Evidently, the lives of the rich and famous are not what they appear to be. "*What the eyes see is better than what the soul desires. This too is futility and a striving after wind.*" (Ecclesiastes 6:9 NASB) Suppose I am headed down a dead end road and meet a car coming back out. The other driver stops and says, "Don't waste your time; there's nothing down this road." There would be no point in my driving several miles to the end of the road anyway only to come to the same conclusion. If riches do not satisfy and the rich tell us so, and God tells us so, there's no point in going down the road of pursuing it when we will come to the same conclusion. The problem is: we'll waste many years doing so. Let's learn to be content in life with what God gives us and set our love on the things that do satisfy: our spouses, our children, and opportunity to do good and the joy of bringing honor to God.

In Moses' case, he not only declined the riches, he willingly accepted the reproaches. He was under no illusions of stepping into a glorious life and into the limelight of praise. He would incur the wrath of all Egypt and the resentment of all Israel before it was over. These are the reproaches of

Christ. He did not count them as a cross or a bitter cup; rather he esteemed these reproaches great riches. He regarded these painful elements of his faith better than the best treasures of the world. How could he do this? "*He had respect unto the recompense of the reward.*" He believed that God would be his "*exceeding great reward.*" God does not reward a rich indulgent life, but he does reward those who willingly deny themselves for the sake of the kingdom of God. There are today untold numbers of folks who extend the use of an older car or content themselves to live in a modest home so that they can afford to give more to missions or other works of the gospel. Why do they do this? Out of love for a Savior who redeemed and renewed them and because they have "*respect unto the recompense of the reward.*" And they shall be rewarded, some thirty-fold, some sixty, some a hundred.

What a lot of us do is try to get the best of both worlds: with one hand we serve God; with the other hand we increase our own riches. Yet in verse 27, we see that Moses "*forsook Egypt*", meaning he abandoned Egypt with no intention of going back. "*No man having put his hand to the plow and looking back is fit for the kingdom of God.*" (Luke 9:62) Too many of us try to keep diplomatic ties with Egypt, just in case things don't work out with God in charge. But how was Moses able to make such a permanent disconnect? "*By faith…he endured as seeing him who is invisible.*" We too can forsake our Egypt, have those old things pass away, refuse to be called the son of Pharaoh's daughter, refuse the pleasures of sin which are but for a season and take up our cross when, by faith, we look unto Jesus, the author and finisher of our faith. It is He who shall, in our wilderness journey, refresh us with living water, feed us with manna from heaven and preserve us from our enemies. Incidentally, there was no manna in Egypt, no shekinah glory, no pillar of fire, and no glorious encounters with God, as at Sinai. Maybe the food and accommodations were a little better in Egypt, but it was not to be compared with the adventures the people of God had in the wilderness. It's the same today.

Too many of us try to keep diplomatic ties with Egypt, just in case things don't work out with God in charge.

Hebrews 13:5
Let your conversation (manner of life) be without covetousness, and be content with such things as you have; for he has said, 'I will never leave you, nor forsake you'.

This is no new command. At Mt. Sinai, God wrote with his own finger, "*Thou shalt not covet.*" Let's not misread this, "Thou shalt not have any fun or enjoyment in life." On the contrary, this commandment was written to enhance our happiness. Why should we desire what we might not ever get? And if we do get the object of our desire, it will not satisfy very much or very long. Coveting is rather like an addiction: there is a "high" of pleasure when we first get some desire of our heart. But all too soon, it does not satisfy any longer, if our heart is still covetous. We hunger for more and better. It is so easy to get ensnared in the cycle of covetousness. What is the solution? Glad you asked. This verse gives a dual answer.

First, ***"be content with such things as you have."*** Happiness need not be linked to the valuation of our possessions. We can choose to be content with little or be discontent with much. God's word is saying be happy with what you have, whether little or much. We *can* do what we *must* do. If we cannot be content with what we have, then we will never be content, for our heart will be always set on what we do not have. This does not forbid ambition to provide good things for our families. But ambition can be tricky; there is but a thin shade of difference between ambition and greed. The expression is simply saying, be content in whatever state you are in. That way, you will always be happy.

We *can* do what we *must* do.

Second, we have such a vast treasure available to us that is able to satisfy us to the core. ***"I will never leave you, nor forsake you."*** When we come to love the Lord our God with all our heart, so much else in life becomes irrelevant.

> *"Turn your eyes upon Jesus*
> *Look full in his wonderful face*
> *And the things of earth will grow strangely dim*
> *In the light of his glory and grace."*

Not only can God be our joy and delight, he is also our provider. He will surely supply our every need. He can supply a whole lot more for us than money can. In him, we may be perfectly content. He would like for us to be.

James 2:5
Hearken, my beloved brethren, Has not God chosen the poor in this world to be rich in faith and heirs of the kingdom which he has promised to them that love him?

This verse must be very disturbing to those who are wealthy. But it need be no more troubling to them than *"a rich man shall hardly enter the kingdom of heaven."* Not only does scripture give needful admonitions to the rich, but it gives helpful encouragements to the poor. As much as this verse may be disturbing to the rich, it must be heartening to the poor. Those who have little in this life seem to be more inclined to hear the gospel and value heavenly reward. Just as we would choose the most fertile ground for our garden, so God chooses the poor in whom to plant his gospel, because the poor are not so much entangled with the *"care of this world and the deceitfulness of riches."* But the wealthy and exalted may also be rich in faith, though it may be more difficult for them. The shepherds were expressly invited to visit the newborn Messiah, but the magi (presumably wealthy) also came later.

Let the poor beware that they do not become too self-assured by this verse as if their poverty guaranteed them eternal life. On the other hand, let the rich develop a healthy rivalry so that they will not allow themselves to be left behind in faith, though they are handicapped with a disadvantage.

James 4:2,3

2. ***You lust, and have not; you kill, and desire to have, and cannot obtain; you fight and war, yet you have not, because you ask not.***
3. ***You ask, and receive not, because you ask amiss, that you may consume it upon your lusts.***

We all lust, and will lust to the last. Taming this tiger is one of the biggest challenges of life. Lust is an excessive or obsessive desire for what we do not have. We use the word today almost exclusively in a sexual context, but it can apply to a broad range of desires. We can lust for a new car or big screen TV. "Lust" comes from the Greek word *epithumeo,* while the Greek word for "covet" is *epithumia.* These two verbs are virtually interchangeable. Thus, we have the New Testament equivalent of "*Thou shalt not covet.*"

This passage depicts the sad plight of man. From the two year old screaming from the grocery cart for some colorful toy to the businessman who sighs with desire at the sight of sprawling country ranch, we lust and have not. When we lust, we are not happy. Paradoxically, we may have been content enough before we saw and lusted with our eyes.

Once lust is loosed, we soon start conniving how we might get what we want. ***"You kill, and desire to have."*** The mafia would kill somebody else to get what they want; the rest of us would all but kill ourselves.

Sometimes our greatest efforts are unsuccessful, and we turn to more devious means: ***"you fight and war."*** So much conflict and misery arise out of our inordinate, misplaced desires. Too many forfeit faith, friendships, family and future to satiate that demon of lust within. This may go on for years, yet all the while God is ready to give to us for the asking. ***"You have not, because you ask not."*** How kind is our God! However, God does not give us a blank check as if we could get anything we want by simply asking Him for it. Some folks get that idea by misapplying such promises as *"Ask and it shall be given to you"* and *"Ask and you shall receive that your joy may be full."* God, like any good father reserves the right to veto any request that would not be good for his child. This is implied in *"No good thing will he withhold from them that walk uprightly."* (Psalm 84:11) He may, however, defer it, and he probably expects us to make formal request for it in prayer. If we are wise and good enough to ask only for good things, we may be sure God will not deny us. We may also be sure that he would not give anything harmful to his child. Jesus explained it this way, *"If a son shall ask bread of any of you that is a father, will he give him a stone?...If you then, being evil, know how to give good gifts unto your children, how much more shall your heavenly Father give the Holy Spirit to them that ask him?"* (Luke 11:11,13) He will give us things that are good for us, such as the Holy Spirit. It's our responsibility to learn what the good things are.

"You ask and receive not, because you ask amiss." I suppose a lot of our requests fall into this class. If we lust too much for worldly possessions, the last thing we need is to feed that lust by having too much: ***"that you may consume it upon your lusts."*** We must starve our sinful appetites, subdue lust within us, crucify the old nature, cast down vain imaginations and realign misplaced affections. We're not going to get anywhere on this list if our praying is too cluttered with requests for possessions, pleasure, money and success.

We must beware that we do not become obsessive in our praying for unwholesome desires. Sometimes God grants in anger what he once refused us in his kindness. If we ask and ask and ask and still receive not, it may be time to reconsider whether the request is scripturally proper. Asking amiss can get us in trouble.

Sometimes God grants in anger what he once refused us in his kindness.

James 5:1-5

1. ***Go to now (Come now), you rich men, weep and howl for your miseries that shall come upon you,***
2. ***Your riches are corrupted and your garments are moth eaten.***
3. ***Your gold and silver are (rusted), and the rust of them shall be a witness against you, and shall eat your flesh as it were fire. You have heaped treasure together for the last days.***
4. ***Behold, the hire of the laborers who have reaped down your fields, which is of you kept back by fraud, cries; and the cries of them who have reaped are entered into the ears of the Lord of Sabbaoth.***
5. ***You have lived in pleasure on the earth, and have been wanton; you have nourished your hearts, as in a day of slaughter.***

This passage is about as popular among the well to do as James 2:5. Though it may seem that these verses utterly castigate the wealthy, they, on the contrary, do a fine service to them in issuing fair warning. Scripture is unapologetic in its rebukes. So should we be. *"He that rebukes a man will afterwards find more favor than he who flatters with his tongue."* (Proverbs 28:23) God has not the least anxiety for how man judges His word. Man better beware the day when God's word shall judge him. In these five verses, God gives us the answers to the test. Here are the standards by which the wealthy will be judged in the last day. We are told in advance, so that we may comply with the word of God and be judged favorably. Verse one shows the alternative -

"Weep and howl for your miseries that shall come upon you." This is that time when there shall be *"weeping and gnashing of teeth"*, and when men shall hear *"you wicked and slothful servant"* and *"depart from me, all you workers of iniquity."* Such eternal sentences will be branded into the consciences of countless souls and shall torment their minds for an eternity. Many will likely flog their own consciences with regrets of having heard and read such admonitions in these former times, and yet did not comply with them. It is not the hearers of the word that are justified, but the doers. Verse one is a forewarning to many Americans that their present luxuries will be turned into miseries. Disbelief in or disregard for this warning will not alter the reality and certainty of judgment. Let's analyze these words, or rather, let them analyze us, no matter how much it may sting our consciences. Let us both hear them and do them.

"Your riches are corrupted and your garments are moth eaten." That which we have strived for and that which we prize so highly are our riches and possessions. This was the sole pursuit of our existence: to have wealth and the finest of everything. We so highly value our gains, but God's opinion of them is that they are decayed and moth eaten. The Laodicean church prides themselves in being *"rich and increased with goods"*, but God says they are poor. If our only wealth is in this world, we are poor indeed. Riches of this world are so transitory and satisfy only momentarily and marginally. The holdings of the wealthy are particularly susceptible to this syndrome. Verse four explains.

"Behold, the hire of the laborers who have reaped down your fields, which is of you kept back by fraud, cries; and the cries of them who have reaped are entered into the ears of the Lord of Sabbaoth." If a man comes into wealth by such shameful usage of the poor, God would be just in ordaining that the owner would find himself unable to enjoy his wealth. *"There is an evil which I have seen under the sun, and it is common among men: a man to whom God has given riches, wealth, and honor, so that he wants (lacks) nothing for his soul of all that he desires, yet God gives him not power to eat thereof."* (Ecclesiastes 6:1,2) Why would a wealthy person who has everything his heart could desire be unable to enjoy it? There may be a sort of curse on it depending on how the wealth was obtained. Not only do the mistreated laborers cry out, as the Israelites cried out for the oppression of their Egyptian bondage, but the withheld wages cry out when wrongfully kept back by the owners. This would be *"riches kept for the owners thereof to their hurt."* (Ecclesiastes 5:13) Habakkuk gives us another example of wages crying out: *"Woe to him that covets an evil covetousness to his house, that he may set his nest on high, that he may be delivered from the power of evil! You have plotted shame to your house by cutting off many peoples, and have sinned against your soul. For the stone shall cry out of the wall, and the beam out of the timber shall answer it."* (Habakkuk 2:9-11) What has happened here is that a man, driven by coveting, has built his very nice house and has *"set his nest on high"*, but has done so at the expense of many people. He has sinned against them, but he probably did not know he also sinned against his own soul. His house, his barn, his land, are all haunted with the mourning cries of the wages due to employees and property due to victims whom he has cheated. What is it that rafters and footings purchased with the wages of sin shall say to each other? They shall tell each other of the injustices done and how they were purchased with wages belonging to another man. The haunting words shall find their way into the subconscious of the owner and give him no rest till he finally cries out himself in repentance, *"Behold, Lord, the half of my goods I give to the poor; and if I have taken anything from any man by false accusation, I restore him fourfold."*

Another fault common among the wealthy is that their ***"gold and silver are (rusted)."*** That is, their wealth is idle. It is buried in the earth. It does no good for anyone except its greedy owner. But no tree eats its own fruit and all the spiritual gifts are given by God to *"profit withal"*, which is to say that spiritual gifts are to profit others, never just the holder of the gift. It would seem that God has the same policy regarding his financial gifts: they are for the purpose of profiting others, not just ourselves or our own family. If all of our finances are kept in CDs, stocks and investments so that we are the only ones benefiting from them, then our wealth is idle, and the rust of them shall be witness against us. The irony of this is that when wealth is distributed in love to those who are in need, it shall bring a nice return for the owner, both materially and spiritually, as God decides.

If you think verse 4 is hard on the rich, look at verse 5: ***"You have lived in pleasure on the earth, and have been wanton; you have nourished your hearts, as in a day of slaughter."*** The Bible minces no words. But remember: this strong language of admonition toward the rich is a clear indication that God loves them. *"Whom the Lord loves, he chastens."* If you think God's being a little hard on us here, remember what Jesus once said to Peter, *"Get thee behind me, Satan."* Yet, Jesus loved Peter enough to rebuke him when he needed it.

Well, what is the Bible saying here? "Thou shalt not have any fun?" Not at all. Rather, this is scolding the sort of conduct we see in the prodigal son, who *"wasted his substance with riotous living."* When the rich live largely to feed their own desires and accomplish their own ambitions, they are as a sheep whose habit of overeating only serves to fatten them for the day of their slaughter. Selfishness displaces joy in this life and disposes for judgment in the next. Aggravating the guilt of such is that they eat so luxuriously, while all around them, others languish.

Selfishness displaces joy in this life and disposes for judgment in the next.

Verse 3 shows the severity of the sentence: ***"Your gold and silver are (rusted), and the rust of them shall be a witness against you, and shall eat your flesh as it were fire. You have heaped treasure together for the last days."*** Some of the wealthy feel exempt from judgment and immune to suffering, so that this warning must seem shocking to them. Their money is a shield from such things: *"the rich man's wealth is his strong city."* (Proverbs 10:15) We have here a basis of the measure of punishment for those who are selfish with their property. By how much the gold, or possessions in general, are *"rusted"*, the owner shall be punished in the next life. They shall be presented as evidence in court that their wealth had done no good. This shall be counted against them, *"shall be a witness against you."* Now this is not the wealth of daily subsistence which a man needs to provide for his household. This is rather gold laid up, stored away, which did neither good for the owner nor anybody else. By how much it is rusted, it shall appear how long the gold lay idle. The Holy Spirit warns us that this very rust shall eat at the flesh (and probably at the consciences) of its owners. The more it is rusted, the more fire there shall be. The more we rob God or sinfully neglect suffering humanity, the more we will suffer through eternity. I have the feeling that the damned shall be made to feel the longings of those whom they denied, the grief of those who suffered loss at their hand, the hunger of those they should have fed, etc. All the treasure some have heaped up for themselves, will ironically become evidence against them. *"Men and brethren, what shall we do?"* To escape these things, we need to repent of our coveting, be converted from our selfish materialism and turn to Jesus Christ as our Master and Forgiver. All who thus call upon him (and only those who call upon him) will be exonerated from the judgment to come.

II Peter 2:15

Who have forsaken the right way, and are gone astray, following the way of Balaam, the son of Beor, who loved the wages of unrighteousness.

What is the *"way of Balaam"*? Or, for that matter, who is Balaam? He is a potent prophet found in Numbers, whose help was solicited against the people of Israel. Balak, king of the Moabites, was fearful that the nearby Israelites might attack them, so he tried to hire or bribe Balaam to curse Israel. He had heard that every word that Balaam spoke came to pass. But God warned Balaam and would not let him speak a curse against Israel. In fact, Balaam pronounced blessing upon them instead, much to the chagrin of King Balak. Not long after this incident, Balaam counseled the Midianites to seduce some of the Israelites into idolatry and harlotry. This resulted in God punishing Israel with a plague in which twenty-four thousand died. Balaam was pretty shrewd in a sinful way. We learn from Moses in Deuteronomy that Balaam was hired for pay in one or both of these incidents: *"they hired against you Balaam, the son of Beor, of Pethor of Mesopotamia, to curse you."* (Deuteronomy 23:4) So the *"way of Balaam"* is to be available for hire to do evil or to counsel to do evil. We may say that Ahithophel went the *"way of Balaam"*, for he was hired to give counsel to wicked Absalom against David. Likewise with Tertullus, who was apparently hired by the high priest and elders to prosecute a case against the apostle, Paul. Two of these three men did their dirty work under the guise of religion. So to go in the way of Balaam is to love getting paid to do evil, especially in the name of religion. We must all be wary of this temptation. How easily we can compromise our faith for more income, or take on an appearance of Godliness for the sake of gain.

I John 2:15,16

15. ***Love not the world, neither the things that are in the world. If any man love the world, the love of the Father is not in him.***

16. ***For all that is in the world, the lust of the flesh, and the lust of the eyes, and the pride of life, is not of the Father, but is of the world.***

This is a much repeated theme throughout the Bible. Yet the message is as clear here as anywhere. This is not our heavenly Father trying to make desert hermits of us all; rather our loving Father, seeing the futility of setting our hearts on that which is doomed to disappoint, teaches us to set our affection on that which is sure to bring lasting happiness.

We are commanded not to love this world; that is, this life and this system and economy, which is catered almost entirely to our carnal appetites. We must not love so much that which this world system consists of, such as power, dominion, admiration, pleasures, etc. Nor must we love objects that are utterly unworthy of our affections like late model cars, high powered PCs, or designer clothing. We must not love even things that are seeming necessities as land, homes and furnishings. These are not bad things. But an object of our love does not have to be bad for it to be bad to love the object. It can be bad for us to love a good object, if loving it tends to be bad *for* us. God gives us his holy laws for our good – our long term good. For example, I once had a neighbor who owned a mint condition black Dodge Charger that was about a twenty-five year old model at the time. It was pretty obvious he really loved that car. He spent nearly two hours per day of quality time with his car in the driveway. When he wasn't tweaking something under the hood, he was cleaning and waxing the body. He also had a wife and a fine little four year old son. Numerous times I would see the wife or the son come outside to be with him. He usually gave them the brush off.

He would shoo the son inside or pay no attention to his wife's attempts at conversation. He seemed to caress his car with loving affection that should have been for his family. I wanted to shake him and say, "Hey, Buster, forget your stupid car! You've got a wife and child who need your love." This is what God is saying to us here. "Love not the car, love not the yacht, love your family, your neighbor and love me – your heavenly Father." Worldly love and spiritual love are mutually exclusive or at least contradictory. As long as my neighbor loved his car as he did, he could not or would not love his wife and son. Likewise, "*if any man love the world, the love of the father is not in him.*" At first glance, it may seem that "*the love of the Father*" refers to the love the Father has for someone. Actually, this is more like love *from* the Father shed abroad in our hearts. The Father has put his kind of love in his children who have received his Holy Spirit, with which they in turn love their neighbor in the way and spirit the Father loves them. So the message is: if any man loves the world (which is really a selfish love), he cannot or, at least, does not love with the Father's love, which is a giving love.

Verse 16 gives three categories of worldly love which contradict the love of the Father, the spiritual love. First...

"The lust of the flesh." To lust is to have excessive, inordinate, or misdirected desire. What may be proper desire to feel for one's spouse would be lust if the desire were toward someone else. So lust would imply not just the degree, but the direction of one's desires. We are to rein in lustful desires or forbid them from going in the wrong direction. We will be judged not only for our actions, but for the lusts in our minds. Anything that is sinful to do, is sinful to fantasize. "*Lust of the flesh*" would include a wide range of appetites, such as sexual desire, appetite for rich foods, misuse of drugs, etc. More pertinent to our discussion are the other two lusts.

"The lust of the eyes." This is usually the most expensive category.

The reason we want to be wealthy is to buy that which appeals to our eyes. The land is beautiful, the car has good lines, etc. Satan tempted Jesus in this way when he showed him all the kingdoms of this world in a moment of time. The visual appeal must have been powerful. It was the lust of the eyes that Emperor Nebuchadnezzar worked to satisfy in all his exploits. He lived for the moment he could say, *"Is not this great Babylon, that I have built for the house of the kingdom by the might of my power, and for the honor of my majesty?"* (Daniel 4:30) Lust of the eyes goes beyond an appreciation of beauty. It greedily desires to have what is appealing to the eye, no matter what the cost or moral consequence. Much of the reason we work so hard to get wealthy is to gratify this lust of the eyes. This is a self-serving gratification that does little good for others. Lust of the eyes is close cousin to ...

"The pride of life." This might look exactly like the lust of the eyes in how it works out in action, but the motive would be a little different. One man might buy a Lexus because it's the best looking car on the market in his mind. The next man might buy an identical car just so he could say he drives a Lexus. The first man acted on the lust of the eyes; the second on the pride of life. In both cases, their action was self-serving and in both cases, it was the reason they worked to become wealthy.

The pride of life may be illustrated by the man who married a very wealthy woman. Things worked out fine since the man did not have to work and the woman had everything she wanted. But the woman had a bad habit of letting everyone know how wealthy she was. As they sat in their luxurious living room one day, she exclaimed how magnificent was the huge living room. Then she said, "If it wasn't for my money, this wouldn't be here." Then she looked out the window at the expensive cars in their driveway and said, "If it wasn't for my money, none of those cars would be here." The husband rolled his eyes, but said nothing. Then the wife strolled to the back window overlooking the swimming pool and tennis courts and the sprawling acreage behind their home. Again she said, "If it wasn't for my money, none of this would be here." Finally the husband blurted out, "If it wasn't for your money, *I* wouldn't be here." We tend to gloat and glory over possessions and positions. When we love having much possessions, much power and much control, we probably are infected with the pride of life. This sort of misplaced affection is not of the Father, but is of the world. May God help each of us to see whether we are guilty of this and deliver us from such evil.

I John 3:17

But whosoever has this world's goods, and sees his brother have need, and shuts up his bowels of compassions from him, how dwells the love of God in him?

We are indeed our brother's keeper. It is apparently a design of God that we will always have rich and poor. Why is that? So that we will always have opportunity to give and share and express compassion. We mature spiritually when we do so. Those of us who have ought not to resent our obligation to care for those in need around us. Giving of ourselves can be very enjoyable and doing so makes us great gainers also. *"Give and it shall be given to you...good measure."*

"And sees his brother have need" There is no question of *whether* we will see our brother in need; the only question is what we will do about it. *"Brother"* may be taken three ways: first, brothers in the flesh. That is, having the same parents. We have a particular obligation to our flesh and blood family. *"But if any provide not for his own, and specially for those of his own house, he has denied the faith, and is worse than an infidel."* (I Timothy 5:8) *"Those of his own house"* would be a man's immediate family, his wife and children, for whom he is morally obligated to care for. A second category given in this verse, *"his own"*, would correspond to his extended family, or his own relatives. This puts somewhat less of an obligation on a man to care for, say, his sister or brother when they come to be in hard times. This general obligation to relatives is also acknowledged in I Timothy 5:4 *"But if any widow have children or nephews, let them learn first to show piety at home, and to requite their parents."* Or their aunt, or sister, etc.

The second way *"brother"* may be taken is in the Christian sense. All who are born again into the family of God may be counted as brothers and sisters in Christ. We should do good to all men, but especially to these who are of the household of faith. Churches ought to take care of their own. The people within a church have a spiritual as well as a social union, and therefore a dual obligation to each other. We ought to regard their burdens as partly our burden, just as we would want the church to come to our assistance when our burdens are particularly heavy. Third, *"brother"* may be taken in the universal sense. That is, all the human race may be considered brothers and sisters in the sense that we are all created by the same God and in the same image. We are also all descended from the same parents, Adam and Eve (and Noah and his wife, too, for that matter). If we have no relationship with someone in need to stir up our compassion, we ought to at least have *"bowels of compassion"* since they are flesh and blood as we are, hurt and suffer as we do, and have aching and longings just as we have. Our compassion ought to move us to sympathize with their feelings and empathize with their position, for we either have been where they are or could easily come to be.

Our compassion should not be confined to our own, our own kin, our own race, our own denomination. May our love and compassion become as widespread and universal as God's.

Conclusion.

This wraps up chapter six. This is certainly not an exhaustive, complete study of everything the apostles had to say on the subject of wealth, but it is hoped that you have learned enough here to catch the drift of what the New Testament teaches. We have heard from Paul, James, John, Peter, Luke, Jude and the writer of Hebrews. Collectively, these men, who knew Jesus best and whom Jesus best enabled to represent him, have conveyed to us the mind of Christ. What they wrote, being moved by the Holy Ghost, is as much an oracle of God as when His voice thundered frightfully across the Sinai wilderness, *"I am the Lord thy God...Thou shalt not covet."* Let us therefore give earnest heed to these things.

"If therefore you have not been faithful in the unrighteous mammon, who will commit to your trust the true riches?"

Luke 16:11

7

May A Christian Be Rich?

"If therefore you have not been faithful in the unrighteous mammon, who will commit to your trust the true riches?" (Luke 16:11) What is Jesus saying? What is the difference between *"unrighteous mammon (wealth)"* and *"true riches"*? We can find answers in the surrounding text. This verse is the concluding theme of the parable of the unjust steward. Remember, that's the guy who was given a sort of two weeks notice that he'd be fired. So to make sure he had friends when he needed them, he called in his master's debtors and wrote off parts of their debt. (It was probably this kind of dishonesty that got the man fired.) Now the main point of the parable is that the steward knew that he'd soon be gone from his current position and made provision for his future state. He did so by making wise (though unscrupulous) use of what he had at hand.

The moral of the story is that we also ought to make provision for our future state since we will not be here long. We may do so by wise use of what we have at hand. Barnabas sold his land and laid the money at the apostles' feet. Cornelius gave *"much alms to the people"*. Both of these men received some of those *"true riches"* now in this time and in the world to come eternal life. (Mark 10:30) Where their treasure went, their heart soon followed.

I. What are True Riches?

Now let's define some terms: first, ***"unrighteous mammon (wealth)"***. Jesus makes it pretty clear that this is money. But why would Jesus be so disparaging of money which is an a-moral object – neither good nor bad? It could be because so many make unrighteous use of money (as the unjust steward). Or it could be because so many get it by unrighteous means. There is not much crookedness or crime that money does not have some connection with. *"The love of money is the root (cause, goal, motivation, instigation) of all (sorts or degrees of) evil."* (I Timothy 6:10) It has been the downfall and damnation of so many, that we should be sharply wary of it. Peter's *"thy money perish with thee"* is an often fulfilled prophecy.

Five times "money" is referred to in the New Testament as "lucre". All five times it is expressed "filthy lucre". Money is as potent to infect our hearts with evil as our hands with germs.

"True riches." While Scripture puts a warning label on *"unrighteous mammon,"* it puts every commendation on *"true riches."* Yet guess which one man seeks most? We will seek most what we value most. *"True riches"* are simply heavenly treasure. Treasure from heaven. Our treasure *in* heaven. *"Treasure in the heavens that fails not." "Riches in glory."* (Luke 12:33 & Philippians 4:19)

Now what does Jesus mean that we are to be *"faithful in the unrighteous mammon?"* In the previous verse, he calls it being *"faithful in that which is least"*. In the following verse, he calls it being *"faithful in that which is another man's"*. Jesus illustrates what he means in his parable. Being *"faithful in unrighteous mammon"* is being faithful to God, the true owner, in our use of the wealth he entrusted to us. First, we are to regard possessions as God's property over which we are made stewards. Second, we are to invest our Master's wealth, so that He gets gain. *"He must increase."* His kingdom must come, his will be done, not ours. The centurion was faithful in unrighteous mammon when he built a synagogue for the Jews. So were the Philippians in their support of Paul. So are we when we support gospel ministries or when we *"strengthen the hand of the poor and needy".* (Ezekiel 16:49)

It is interesting that only in Philippians is such an assurance found, *"For my God shall supply all your need according to his riches in glory by Christ Jesus".* (Philippians 4:19) For it was only the church at Philippi who continued to support Paul's work even after he left the region. *"For even in Thessalonica, you sent once and again unto my necessity."* (Philippians 4:16) Notice the Philippians were faithful in unrighteous mammon, faithful in that which is least, faithful in that which is another man's. So will they receive *"true riches"*? Paul says "yes". They are sure to receive *"riches in glory",* not merely filthy lucre.

It seems to me that Philippians 4:19 is one of the most mis-applied verses in the Bible. This promise is to Philippian grade Christians who support the gospel, support their church, pay their tithes. Notice also that no guarantee is given (at least not here) that those who are faithful in unrighteous mammon are sure to get more of it. The promise is that tithing, Philippian Christians will receive *"riches in glory",* such riches as come when the windows of heaven are opened. Riches like a gratifying marriage, gold nuggets for preaching, the power of God in one's life; things we wouldn't trade for a million dollars.

Granted, financial increase may also come, but it is only corollary to the main gift as it was for Solomon. *"And I have also given you that which you have not asked, both riches and honor."* (I Kings 3:13) It is probably safe to say that if the motive for tithing is to get more money (as if God were some kind of investment strategy), no deal. This would be using God to serve money. Tithing or praying in order to get more money sounds like evidence that a person is not ready for it. This is *"asking amiss"* and, no doubt, would be consumed upon their lust.

It is probably safe to say that if the motive for tithing is to get more money (as if God were some kind of investment strategy), no deal.

There are not too many Christians who can be rich – safely, that is. *"Not many noble are called."* (I Corinthians 1:26) May a Christian be rich? I can just hear God say, "Wrong question number 101." Maybe the right question would be, "Why would a Christian want to be rich?" Shall a Christian, of all people, heed this call of the sirens – *"the deceitful of riches"*? Why would a Christian heap to themselves that which was the death of Judas, the distraction of Demas, the demise of Laodicea, and the damnation of *"a certain rich man"*?

Above all else, God wants to commit to our trust *"true riches"*. But we demonstrate ourselves unworthy of them when our heart is set on earthly riches. In fact, that would also make us unworthy of earthly riches.

Paradoxically, it seems that the only Christians fit to be rich are those who have no heart for it. They would surely be best suited to be stewards of it. It would be safest for one to handle such a dangerous commodity who was immune to it. It's a good thing I don't drive a pastry delivery truck. Both the pastries and I would soon be in trouble. I would probably be a poor steward of the goods delivered to me.

The goods and assets in our possession are not for us to consume, but to distribute. If we fail to do so, we bring trouble upon ourselves. *"There is a sore evil which I have seen under the sun, namely, riches kept for the owners thereof to their hurt."* (Eccles. 5:13)

A Christian *may* be rich when they are safe from the hazard of it. A Christian *may* be rich when they have no appetite for consuming the wealth themselves. A Christian *may* be rich when their heart is set on building the kingdom of God, relieving the poor, strengthening the church, visiting the fatherless and widows in their affliction. God does not give us wealth purely for our enjoyment. We are to judiciously distribute it for our Master's gain. *"Lord, thy pound has gained ten pounds."*

"But it's *my* money. I worked hard for it." We may have planted and watered, but God gave the increase. We may have worked, but God gave the golden opportunities. Check and see if it wasn't God who gave you favor with the right people as He gave Daniel favor with the prince over him.

"But I worked in school and got a degree to get a good job." Again, check and see if it wasn't God who *gave* you the necessary knowledge as with Daniel, *"As for these four...God gave them knowledge and skill in all learning."* (Daniel 1:17) If we are humble enough to give due credit to God, there's not much left for us to take credit for.

Haven't we all seen smart, capable men struggling financially, while sometimes simple, easy-going folks come into sizeable wealth? *"The race is not always to the swift...nor yet riches to men of understanding."* (Ecclesiastes 9:11) God is sovereign; He decides.

II. Is It God's Will for Me to Be Rich?

The doctrine that God wants us to be healthy and wealthy is widespread and understandably popular. This teaching is found in many denominations and in all regions of the United States. But I suppose it's not so popular abroad.

Preachers from some of the finest fabric of our society skillfully deliver this message of "health and wealth". No doubt, they mean well. Preachers love their people and want to see them prosper. This is a valid point, but some caution is in order. It is important to avoid extremes. One extreme is being obsessed with riches. The other is not working at all.

The Bible is not very complimentary of people who will not even provide for the basic necessities of their family. *"But if any provide not for his own, and especially for those of his own house, he has denied the faith and is worse than an infidel."* (I Timothy 5:8)

Some need this admonition. We do well to kindle a little initiative in those where it's lacking. They should take to heart the words of the Lord Jesus, *"It is more blessed to give than to receive"* and so labor as to support the weak. We are also to *"requite our parents"* and honor our father and mother in caring for them when it's their turn.

The extreme of being obsessed with riches is the more common problem today and maybe the more deadly. Whatever the intentions of "Health and Wealth" proponents, the effect is far too often that gullible Christians set their affections and ambitions on material gain. This is a "feel good" gospel in which our flesh (our worldly nature) delights. Such preaching tickles our ears and tickles our fancy. Acquisition of wealth, possessions or power directly feeds the fleshly appetite. This puts the flesh in dominance over the Spirit within us. So in this extreme, we must beware of getting too much of a good thing.

So is it God's will for me to be rich? Think of it this way: if the answer is "yes", does it apply to me, or does it apply equally to Christians in China, South Africa or Venezuela? Does God want just me to be rich? Or just Americans? Or just Baptists or Pentecostals? What makes me so special? We know God loves all his children equally. So if he wants me to be blessed with wealth, then he would surely want the same for his beloved children around the world. It makes sense that he would want us blessed equally. It logically follows that he would want those of us who have more to share with those who have less. *"As it is written, He that had gathered much had nothing over; and he that had gathered little had no lack."* (II Corinthians 8:15) How can we justify living like kings and queens when so much of the world suffers lack?

Part of the problem with a Christian being rich is that they *want* to be rich. This is a very unhealthy sign. *"But they that will (wish to) be rich fall into temptation and a snare, and into many foolish and hurtful lusts, which drown men in destruction and perdition."* (I Timothy 6:9) Just the desire to be rich is a strong indication that the heart is not with God. *"If any man loves the world, the love of the Father is not in him."* (I John 2:15) According to God's Word, coveting or loving money amounts to *"erring from the faith"*.

Getting back to the question: "may a Christian be rich?", it might be easier to address it by dividing it into three parts:

A. ***How* did the Christian get rich?**
B. **What does the Christian do with his wealth?**
C. **What does the wealth do with the Christian?**

The first question addresses the Christian's integrity in acquiring his wealth. Obviously, ill-gotten gains would not be God's will. So it's important to ask –

III. *How* Did the Christian Get Rich?

When I was in Bible college, I talked with a young medical doctor who had received Christ about a week before we met. He related to me some investment schemes he was involved in concerning the import/export business. As we discussed the matter, it became clear that there were some questionable ethics involved. I asked him, "What would Jesus say about this?" He grinned at me and said, "I think I need to get out of this business." I agreed with him.

It's a "no-brainer" that wealth obtained by outright dishonesty or trickery is wrong. But a problem arises when *we* draw the line between right and wrong. We would certainly include our own practices within the boundary of what is right. "*All the ways of a man are clean in his own eyes, but the Lord weighs the spirits.*" (Proverbs 16:2) We are never more merciful, forgiving and gracious than when we are judging ourselves. So we have to be honest here. Another problem with judging ourselves is that we gladly allow testimony for the defense, but not for the prosecution. An interesting test would be to poll the opinion of everyone with whom we do business. How would they judge our fairness and business ethics? (Maybe this is not such a good idea after all.)

Another problem with judging ourselves is that we gladly allow testimony for the defense, but not for the prosecution.

Suppose a Christian leases or sells a house. How does he decide how much to ask for it? Of course, there's a "bottom line" he must get to avoid losing money. Then there's the maximum amount he could get if he demanded it and held out long enough. Without hesitation, most go for the highest amount they can get. The justification is: "Well nobody's forcing them to buy it or rent it. If they don't want it, they can find another house." But in most cases, the owner could make a comfortable profit by reducing the price considerably. For many families, even a small reduction would be a huge relief financially. God surely takes favorable notice of landlords, doctors, repairmen and creditors who are particularly merciful and easy on the elderly, poor folks and single moms. (And in some cases, single Dads.)

One mechanic in our church recently performed some fairly expensive repairs on the rather modest vehicle of a single mother. He charged nothing for his own labor, even though the mechanic was himself in financial straits. He and his wife and five children were down to one operative car. His own truck had been stranded for two months, needing a $1200.00 transmission. He was unable to get a loan. Shortly after repairing the single mother's car at no cost, a truck identical to his own came up for sale. He was able to buy the other truck for $500.00 and transfer the transmission to his own truck. He also salvaged a number of other parts from the other truck which his truck needed. He estimates the total value of other salvaged parts to be about $300.00 – so far. Coincidence, you say? I prefer to pronounce it "providence". Jesus said, *"Blessed are the merciful, for they shall obtain mercy."* (Matthew 5:7)

What a contrast to other mechanics who charge such high fees, you get the impression they're trying to retire on your car. This is like the guy who drove his car into the mechanic's shop for repairs. With just a casual glance at the car, the mechanic said, "Your estimate is $ 642.17." The suspicious owner asked, "How can you possibly be so exact when you hardly even looked at it?" The mechanic replied, "That's the amount of my overdue house note."

You see, we're all quick to criticize others' excesses, but ready to justify our own. We need to fairly address the question: *how* did I get rich? Proverbs 28:20 cautions, *"he that makes haste to be rich shall not be innocent."* Gehazi would retort, "Tell me about it." Judas would concur, "No kidding."

Many might object, "But I'm no Gehazi or Judas. I run an honest business." Do you? Would an I.R.S. audit conclude the same? Would your customers and clients agree with your assessment? Or would the Lord's scrutiny result in *"I have somewhat against you."*

What it comes down to is this sharp-pronged, stinging question: "Am I making a substantial or generous profit at the painful expense of someone else?" Do I *"build up Zion with blood and Jerusalem with iniquity?"* or *"eat the flesh of my people and flay their skin from off them?"* (Micah 3:3,10) Does *"the stone cry out of the wall, and the beam out of the timber"* in protest? *"Woe to him that builds a town with blood."* (Habakkuk

2:11 and 12) Judas isn't the only one who betrayed Christ for money. And Joseph isn't the only brother who was betrayed for money.

Let's pick on store owners next. Suppose the store owner brings home $120,000.00 per year. Most would agree that a person could scrape by pretty comfortably on that kind of income. However, if the employees are struggling to feed their families on minimum wage, then his comforts are somewhat at their expense. A Christian owner might consider giving a $1.00 per hour raise to his employees. If this cuts his gains to $100,000.00 per year, he'd still be doing well and his employees would be happy. The owner would be blessed as Job was: "*The blessing of him that was ready to perish came upon me: and I caused the widow's heart to sing for joy.*" (Job 29:13) In other words, the employees would ask God to bless the boss for his kindness, and God would do it. In fact, God would probably bless the man whether the employees were grateful or not.

Maybe the employees are doing fine, but the owner decides he could afford to moderate his profits by discounting his prices to ease the cost to his customers. This would be giving in good measure and amounts to good security for the future of his business. "*Whatever measure you deal out to others, it will be dealt to you in return.*" (Luke 6:38, NASB) Clearly, this would show the man to be free from the love of money and shows evidence of loving his neighbor as himself, and God above his wealth.

Most would laugh such an idea to scorn. Most owners tweak their businesses to squeeze every last dollar they can out of it. But this is addressed to Christians, not to them. The Bible teaches that there are some things more important than money: "*A good name is rather to be chosen than great riches, and loving favor rather than silver and gold.*" (Proverbs 22:1) Why can't employers have loving favor? When's the last time your employees put on a surprise birthday party for you?

So the question is: **How did the Christian get rich?** If it were by questionable or dishonest means, then it would surely not be the will of

God. (It is no more justifiable if we plan to use the money for charitable causes.) Zaccheus should stand up and say *"Behold, Lord, the half of my goods I give to the poor* (from whom he got it unfairly in the first place) *and if I have taken any thing from any man by false accusation, I restore him fourfold."* (Luke 19:8)

However, in this land of opportunity, there are certainly many who have acquired much by legitimate means. They would clear the first check point and proceed to the second question.

IV. What Does the Christian Do With His Wealth?

The usual choice is to say, *"Soul, you have much goods laid up for many years: take thine ease, eat, drink and be merry"* like the fellow whose ground brought forth plentifully. Sounds innocent enough. *"But God said unto him, 'Thou fool'"*. (Luke 12:20) The explanation is expressed in verse 21, *"So is he that lays up treasure for himself, and is not rich toward God."* Where did this guy go wrong? No mention is made of any dishonest gain. Weren't his goods for him to enjoy? Maybe God was just being a grouch. Notice also that nothing is said about him being greedy, though he certainly was. In the case of dishonesty or greed, God would likely have said, "Thou crook" or "thou covetous". But God precisely dubbed him *"fool"* because he made a foolish, fatal blunder; he did not store up real treasure in heaven. He was spiritually bankrupt. It is foolish to have much regard for (and fatal to have much affection for) transitory, uncertain riches which *"make themselves wings,* (and) *fly away as an eagle"*. (Proverbs 23:5) We tend to think that business shares and real estate are more real than heavenly treasure. Which is more real: the substance of this world which evaporates as quickly as a morning fog, or eternal, imperishable riches, which neither moth nor rust can corrupt nor inflation or stock fluctuations can diminish?

So the fellow in Luke 12 may have acquired his wealth honestly enough, but went wrong by planning to hoard it. This would be a mistake for two reasons. First,

His Wealth Is Idle. It is doing no good for any other than himself. He has buried his talent. But wasn't it his money to do with as he pleases? Not exactly. As in the parable of the talents (Matthew 25:14ff), he was but a steward of God given wealth. Not just the tenth, but the total belongs to the Lord. We who are the bond-servants of the Lord would happily assent to his ownership, not only of our souls, but of our substance. So if we find that our Master has made us steward over somewhat of his possessions, it is our duty to *"trade"* with it and cause increase to His kingdom. We must not think that He gave us so much to *"consume it upon* (our) *lusts"*. (James 4:3)

Not just the tenth, but the total belongs to the Lord.

At work, I am once in a while called upon to deliver payroll checks to 35 fellow employees. Once they've been entrusted to me, it's my duty to deliver the checks to the owners. It is not an option for me to say, "Wow, this is my lucky day! Look how God has blessed me." In the same way, we may assume that if God has entrusted to us the wealth of this world, He intends that we disburse it, not keep it. Imagine how my co-workers would feel if I decided to cash their paychecks and take a Caribbean cruise. There'd be a public lynching when I returned. That's about how God must feel.

When we do not invest what God has entrusted to us in such a way as to cause increase to his kingdom, we have let our talent become idle. The rust of our gold and silver shall be a witness against us. Second,

***He* is idle.** Let's consider also the effect of the wealth on the retiree of Luke 12. It only made him idle. Even if he had lived longer, he would have become lazy, taken his ease, become indulgent, and do little else but eat, drink and be merry. He would surely set his affection on things on the earth, rather than on things above. Worst of all, he would probably have denied the Lord, being full and said, *"Who is the Lord?"* (Proverbs 30:9)

Scripture does not take too kindly to idleness. (Neither did my Dad.) *"Thou wicked and slothful servant..."* (Matthew 25:26) *"Why stand ye here all the day idle?"* (Matthew 20:6)

Remember how David got in trouble with Bathsheba? *"And it came to pass, after the year was expired, at the time when kings go forth to battle, that David sent Joab, and his servants with him and all Israel; and they destroyed the children of Ammon, and besieged Rabbah. But David tarried still at Jerusalem."* (II Samuel 11:1) This is the first time David ever skipped going to war. He was resting on his laurels. *"Shall your brethren go to war and shall you sit here?"* (Numbers 32:6) He was being idle. It gets worse. *"And it came to pass in an eveningtide, that David arose from off his bed."* (II Samuel 11:2) What is the king of Israel doing sleeping all day and getting up in the evening? The king ought to be *"redeeming the time, because the days are evil."* Idle days especially. Behold how idleness is the devil's workshop.

The story continues that David *"walked upon the roof of the king's house: and from the roof he saw a woman washing herself; and the woman was very beautiful to look upon."* Verse 4 reports the shameful outcome: *"and David sent messengers and took her...and he lay with her."* No wonder God doesn't want us idle. Idleness is a sin for anybody. For the poor, because his hands have not ministered to his own necessities, and for the independently wealthy, because *"so laboring they ought to support the weak."* (Acts 20:34,35)

One more thought on idleness may be derived from Ezekiel 16:49, *"Behold, this was the iniquity of your sister, Sodom, pride, fullness of bread, and abundance of idleness was in her and in her daughters, neither did she strengthen the hand of the poor and needy."* Idleness was a breeding ground for the gross abominations Sodom became infamous for. What unprecedented sin might idleness breed in us given the chance?

Lastly, notice an aggravating condition of Sodom's idleness: that those who were idle for having "*fullness of bread*" neglected to use their extra time and wealth to relieve the struggling poor among them. It's one thing to be idle when everybody around is doing fine. But it is a shame for us to take our ease when others are heavy laden.

It is a shame for us to take our ease when others are heavy laden.

Back to the question: **What does the Christian do with his wealth?** Surely God would not want us to squander it all on subsidizing our leisure, like the bumper sticker on the R.V. that says "We're spending our children's inheritance."

However, this does not mean that a Christian should not save up for retirement. We're encouraged to consider the ways of the ant (Proverbs 6:6) which "*provide her meat in the summer, and gathers her food in the harvest*". In other words, the ant stores up for leaner times. So did Joseph in the Egyptian famine. We, too, may store up for retirement so that we may sustain ourselves. However, a Christian should take heed to retire more comfortably, than luxuriously.

What if the Christian accumulates savings to the point where he retires early, or partly, in order to devote himself to the Lord's work at his own expense? Surely God would find this acceptable. This leads us to part three of the question: **May a Christian Be Rich?**

V. What Does the Wealth Do With the Christian?

In general, the wealth we have accumulated seldom does us any good. We think we own the possessions, but practically, they own us. Our estates and assets become tyrants of our time and masters of our mind. The saying is valid: no man is ever really free as long as he owns anything.

Solomon observes, "*the sleep of a laboring man is sweet, whether he eats little or much: but the abundance of the rich will not suffer (allow) him to sleep.*" (Ecclesiastes 5:12) You see, the riches own such a man and dreadfully dominate him. The same preoccupation with profits ruins the vacation of many a company owner and hinders his enjoyment of family time. How many Daddys diddle with business at their child's ball game? Or bring their briefcase on their vacation, or cannot part with their cell phone, named appropriately enough. Some Daddys better wake up and give their child some real attention – while they still want it. Nobody ever says on their death bed, "Gee I wish I'd spent more time at the office."

What does the wealth do with the Christian? Does it fill him with such thoughts as, "Wow, think of all the good I can do with this?" Or does he rather think, "Now where should I invest all this?" Nothing reveals a person's character quite as well as when they come into considerable wealth.

What does the wealth do with the Christian? It usually draws his heart away from God in both affection and reliance. A man's love for his possessions encroaches more and more on his love for God. Inch by inch, wealth steals our heart away from God, as Absalom stole the hearts of Israel away from David. We lose our first love.

The more assets and securities we have, the more we tend to trust in them and the less we rely on God. When we become full, we deny him. (Proverbs 30:9) Wealth can erode a man's faith, chill his Christian zeal and shrivel his love of neighbor. Wealth seldom betters a man, but it often fetters a man. There is no test like prosperity. Witness David, Solomon and the kings of Israel. They became better men in the hard times, but fell into temptation in the prosperous times.

Wealth can erode a man's faith, chill his Christian zeal and shrivel his love of neighbor.

The almost inescapable hazard of wealth is that we become lovers of money. Consider the evil that comes from such a root of misplaced affections. It became a snare for Ananias and Sapphira, who "*kept back part of the price*" and lied to the apostles and God. For the love of money, Gehazi became a leper and Demas an apostate. Love of money set the two brothers of Luke 12:13 against each other. And they aren't the only ones. For the love of money, Felix would not release Paul. "*He hoped also that money should have been given him of Paul, that he might loose him.*" (Acts 24:26) For the love of money, Achan and thirty six innocent men died. Love of money incited Delilah to treachery and Judas to treason.

The love of abundance moved Jezebel to murder, and the sons of Samuel to pervert justice. For the love of money, Shishak, king of Egypt, stole the gold from the temple in Jerusalem. This practice is continued to this day.

It is a well-worn weapon of the Wicked one to tempt us with prosperity. "*All these things will I give thee.*" You may be thinking, "Gee, if it's that dangerous being rich, it'd be better not to be rich." Exactly. In fact, I should have thought of that myself.

It is a solemn question: What does the wealth do with the Christian? May a Christian be rich? Sure, but let him consider whether his wealth is God's blessing or the devil's temptation.

Let a man consider whether his wealth is God's blessing or the devil's temptation.

May a Christian be rich? Yes, but only if he becomes so honestly and fairly. May a Christian be rich? Certainly. However, God intends that we be stewards of his estate, to distribute to the necessity of the saints or the church, or to *"do good unto all men."* (Galatians 6:10)

May a Christian be rich? Yes, but let him understand that the Great Physician has determined that wealth can be hazardous to his soul. It has been known to cause spiritual cancer in rats. You know, those ones in the rat race. Let the Christian who has come into wealth consider the effect it has had on his soul, his walk with God, his relationship with his family or his availability to the church.

Not long ago, I talked with a newlywed couple. The wife was very recently become a Christian, just before their wedding, I believe. The husband, whom I'll call Mickey, had been a Christian several years. He told me of his plans to attend seminary and to possibly go into the ministry. The wife was eager to grow as a Christian and to become active in church. She was happy to have such a learned husband to teach her. There was only one problem: Mickey began to experience phenomenal success in his business. Within a year of organizing, he owned several stores and had over one hundred employees. His income sky-rocketed to nearly $200,000.00 per year. You may be wondering: so where's the problem? The wife expressed to me her frustration that he did not attend church with her. He was not helping her grow in her new found faith. So his pre-occupation with his business was hurting his family and his faith.

Now I'm just guessing, but I wonder if Mickey (and many like him) thought to himself, "Just a little longer building up my company and I'll be able to retire and serve the Lord full time." Sounds very nice. But let me tell you about Frank. A life long Christian, Frank was the owner of a large auto dealership for many years. He worked hard and retired early at fifty-eight years old, a millionaire. For years he had looked forward to that day. He said to himself that when he retired, he'd get back into church and serve God. True to his word, he did so. Frank became a valuable help to his pastor and served God and his church honorably. But Frank died at sixty years old. May a Christian be rich? Yes, but let him not mortgage his faith for his finances!

If Satan cannot work someone's wealth to be their destruction, he'll see to it that it becomes their distraction. *"Some fell among thorns; and the thorns sprang up with it and choked it."* (Luke 8:7) Our minds get so clogged with the *"cares of this world"* and so allured by *"the deceitfulness of riches"*. Notice in this verse how strongly Jesus states the danger: he describes the riches as *"choking"* the owner. This is like the owner of a python. When it is young, it is easily handled. But the bigger it grows, the more difficult it gets to handle. Then one fateful day, the python turns on him, wraps its coils around him and slowly begins choking the life out of the owner. In the end the riches come to "own" the person. As in the case of wine, *"at the last it bites like a serpent and stings like an adder."* (Proverbs 23:32)

It irks me to no end that men will serve their own interests throughout the prime of their life (or the best hours of their day) and then give God their worn out leftovers. Shouldn't we remember our Creator now, in the days of our youth?

It peeves me that many of the best men and the best minds in America go to the fields of finance, law, engineering, business and medicine, rather than to the ministry. Many churches have to settle for the mediocre leftovers. But it is no new thing that *"not many wise men after the flesh, not many mighty, not many noble are called"*. (I Corinthians 1:26)

May a Christian be rich? I guess so. But more pertinently, can the *rich* be *Christian*? That is, can the Christian who has become rich continue in the integrity of his faith? The problem is that rich Christians usually act more rich than Christian. The extravagance of many a wealthy Christian is a puzzle to less fortunate believers. They do not understand how the wealthy Christian could spend so much on themselves with serious needs all around them.

Neither do I. Rare, but pleasant to behold, is the Godly woman or man who maintains their spiritual graces, though they have greatly prospered. Usually, the increasing of gains is the diminishing of graces. Sadly, when we increase, He usually decreases. (John 3:30) It's equally pleasant to see accomplished athletes or attractive ladies who are also adorned with kindness, humility and love. But, alas, it is more the exception than the rule.

Where is the wealthy man or woman who is an equal friend to both the poor and the prominent; who lives with the same moderation they always did; who is as kind and loving and principled as they ever were?

May a Christian be rich? Yes, but let him beware lest he brings upon himself, *"temptation and a snare, and...many foolish and hurtful lusts, which drown men in destruction and perdition."* The appetite for affluence has ruined many a man through gambling, lotteries and risky investments. In the race for riches, countless "successful" businessmen and entrepreneurs have left in their wake, violated values and heartbroken homes.

So many have eaten the forbidden fruit of love of money and pierced themselves through with many sorrows. Let's learn the lesson of Lot, who, in hopes of wealth, eyed the lush green valleys of Sodom and Gomorrah and turned his back on his Godly kin, including Abraham. How much better it would have been for him to say, *"Entreat me not to leave you...for where you go, I will go...your people shall be my people, and your God, my God."* (Ruth 1:16) But sadly, Lot lost everything.

It was for love of money that: Gehazi lost his health and his calling; Judas lost his soul and the rich man fell short of eternal life. For love of money the soldiers lied about the resurrection of Christ; for love of money, men used the poor damsel possessed with the spirit of divination. Love of money makes the Laodicean church neither cold nor hot, so that God is sick of them, and for the love of money, the wrath of God comes upon the children of men. (Ephesians 5:6)

May a Christian be rich? Yes, but let him tremble at the prospect.

"You shall love your neighbor as yourself."

Matthew 22:39

"He that has pity upon the poor lends unto the Lord, and that which he had given will he pay him again."

Proverbs 19:17

How Much Am I My Brother's Keeper?

If you have read this far, either you had to read this for punish work, or you have a heart to live right in the sight of God. In the previous chapters, we saw that the Word of God leaves little latitude for living as we please. We must enter the kingdom of God through the narrow straits of the gospel's compelling demands. Few enough seek the kingdom of God to begin with; even fewer shall actually attain. *"Strive to enter in at the strait gate; for many, I say unto you, will seek to enter in, and shall not be able."* My guess is that of those who have read this far, a sizeable majority are striving to enter in. It is my hope that you've come to understand what Scripture says and now seek how you may comply with it. It is a relief to us that just as the Scripture enlightens our mind with instruction, it also lightens our path with direction. To every humble soul who asks, *"Lord, what will you have me to do?"*, God gives an answer.

It goes without saying that we are to be our brother's keeper, as the good Samaritan was. Christians are called upon to *"support the weak"*, to *"visit the fatherless and widows in their affliction"*, *"to entertain strangers"*, as Abraham and Lot did, to *"distribute to the necessity of the saints"*, as Paul and Barnabas did, and to be *"given to hospitality"*, as Mary and Martha were. God puts this obligation upon those of us who are able: *"and if your brother (becomes) poor, and fallen in decay (poverty) with you; then you shall relieve him: yes, (even) though he be a stranger, or a sojourner.*" (Leviticus 25:35) These are as much a duty to the Christian (or, rather, to all men) as paying our tithes or taxes. Yes, even if we never saw the man before, or owe him nothing, even if the man is wicked and ungrateful, "*for He is kind to the unthankful and to the evil*". Those who refuse to obey this mandate of kindness bring upon themselves the indignation of the Father, as happened to Nabal, the churl. (See I Samuel 25)

There is no question that we are to be our brother's keeper. The question is: How far does this obligation go? First, let's consider how much we should give on the basis of...

I. How Giving Benefits Ourselves.

Jesus said that we shall have the poor with us always. We can think of this as a guarantee of investment opportunity. What we sow is what we reap. We can sow a little kindness and reap more of it in return. We all like to invest for our future. We recognize its uncertainty and like the ant, "*provide (our) meat in the summer, and gather (our) food in the harvest.*" (Proverbs 6:8) Joseph would agree that it makes sense to store up for retirement days or for lean times as he did in Egypt. Yet not so much as the rich man who said, "*Take thine ease, eat, drink and be merry*". (See Luke 12:19)

Most everyone figures that doing good to the poor results in heavenly reward. However, Jesus assures us that our good is rewarded in this life as well: "*Verily, I say unto you, There is no man that has left house, or brothers, or sisters, or father, or mother, or wife, or children, or lands, for my sake, and the gospel's, but he shall receive a hundredfold now in this time, houses, and brethren, and sisters, and mothers, and children, and lands, with persecutions; and in the world to come eternal life.*" (Mark 10:29, 30) The reward is not only *"in the world to come"*, but also *"now in this time"*. The reward is not just spiritual, but also material: *"houses...and lands"*.

God understands that we are but flesh and that heavenly reward is difficult for us to comprehend, and more so to be motivated by. So He accommodates our impatience and grants us a little earnest of our reward in this life. This is like the father who takes his little son out to dinner for steak and lobster at the finest restaurant in town. During the long ride to the restaurant, the son says, "Daddy, can we stop and get a hot dog? I'm hungry *now*." God likewise satisfies our appetite so we don't get discouraged along the way.

Back to Mark 10:30. Most of us leap on the promise that there is reward in this life for our good and put little value on the eternal, more excellent reward. This shows that our affections are set too much on the things of this world, rather than on things above. Forget the steak and lobster, we want our hot dog *now*! We are like Abram when the Lord came to him in a vision and said, *"I am your shield and exceeding great reward."* (Genesis 15:1) Abram seems to put little value on God's friendship when he replies, *"Lord God, what will you give me..."* It must have hurt God's feelings. (Like we do every day.) We undervalue the best things God has provided for us and over-value the least, like the toddler who has more fun with the wrapping paper than the gift.

Such grand promises as we find in Mark 10:30 ought to move us to *"sell (what we) have and give alms"* and *"provide (ourselves) bags which wax not old, a treasure in the heavens that fails not."* (Luke 12:33) There is no more sure investment. Now let's take a look at –

WHAT CONSTITUTES A GOOD INVESTMENT.

Most brokers would agree that a good investment includes:

a. guaranteed returns
b. long term stability
c. investment availability
d. high percentage yield

Now consider how solid an investment charity would be:

A. **Guaranteed returns.** Few investments today can make this promise. Yet Scripture gives us strong assurances of reward to exercisers of charity:
  - *"If you draw out your soul to (if your heart goes out to) the hungry and satisfy the desire of the afflicted soul, then* ***shall*** *your light rise in obscurity... and the Lord* ***shall*** *guide you continually, and satisfy your soul in drought."* (Isaiah 58:10,11)
  - *"But when you do alms...your Father who sees in secret, himself* ***shall*** *reward you openly."* (Matthew 6:3,4)
  - *"Give and it* ***shall*** *be given to you."* (Luke 6:38)
  - *"Then shall the King say to them on His right hand, 'Come you blessed of my Father, inherit the kingdom prepared for you from the foundation of the world: For I was hungry, and you gave me meat: I was thirsty and you gave me drink: I was a stranger, and you took me in.'"* (Matthew 25:34,35)

B. **Long term stability.** Some of the best stocks available could conceivably be wiped out in a day. The best planned developments can easily become losses by a conflicting, detrimental development next door. No investment could weather a total collapse of the U.S. economy or an overthrow of the U.S. government.

Ultimately, there is the final dissolving of every estate or gain in this world by the decease of the owner. So our best investments in this world pay us dividends only to the point of our death. Beyond that, they cannot avail for us even a drop of water.

However, charity is one investment that truly does have long term stability. This is likewise true for investing a little kindness or supporting the gospel ministry. For God Himself is the rewarder and *"His dominion is an everlasting dominion and His kingdom is from generation to generation."*

Thus the reward for those who choose to be their brother's keeper is eternal. We already discussed that the reward is not only eternal, but temporal. Proverbs 11:31 asserts, *"the righteous shall be recompensed* ***in the earth****"*. No one who invests in Godliness shall be losers at any time. *"Godliness with contentment is great gain"*, steady gain, lasting gain.

C. **Investment availability.** Although some investments are available to only a few, the best one is available to all. We may make heavenly deposits anywhere, anytime. One Christian made such a deposit when he noticed a humbly dressed man with crutches napping on a public bench. When the man awoke, he found a five dollar bill wedged into his crutch, never knowing where it came from.

   Most of the time, though, we make weekly deposits into our heavenly accounts at church or by regular support of a struggling relative. Opportunities are endless in scope and variety and can be lots of fun. A short term missionary in the Philippines visiting a work north of Manila observed numerous young children in the neighborhood. When business required a trip to town, he stocked up. Upon returning, he gave away assorted balls to each of about twenty-five little boys and colored hair barrettes to about as many little girls. It probably cost him no more than fifty dollars, but he surely had more fun than a barrel of monkeys in a banana patch.

We are not guaranteed a place in heaven just because we do good.

Something vitally important must be said about this "investment availability" concept. Although the opportunity to invest a little charity toward others is available to everyone, we don't all have deposit accounts in heaven. Let me explain. We are not guaranteed a place in heaven just because we do good. Ephesians 2:8 and 9 make this clear: *"For by grace are you saved through faith; and that not of yourselves: it is the gift of God: not of works, lest any man should boast."*

We are not saved by our own efforts, *"not of yourselves"*, or by doing good, *"not of works"*. Rather, the saving of our soul is a joint effort of God and the person. First, the *"grace"* of God or the *"gift of God"* is offered to every person. God's condescending love is available to *"whosoever will call upon the name of the Lord"*. Those who believe in God accept His gift by faith. So man's faith trusts in God's grace and accepts God's gift. What gift? The gift of eternal life, which includes:

- unconditional pardon
- receiving the Holy Spirit
- receiving a new nature (being born again)
- assurance of heaven
- eternal life
- being adopted as a child of God
- being declared legally righteous

Now once we have eternal life, we have a place in heaven and it can then be said we have an "account" there. Only then do our good works merit us a heavenly reward. *"Their works do follow them."*

Many American church-goers are not aware of this. Indeed Jesus warned that many church-goers will fall short of heaven. *"Many will say to me in that day (the judgment day), Lord, Lord have we not prophesied in thy name? And in thy name have cast out devils? And in thy name done many wonderful works? And then I will profess unto them, I never knew you: depart from me you that work iniquity."* (Matthew 7:22,23)

So we must accept the gift of God before *our* gift becomes acceptable with Him. Our good works must have the acceptable aroma of Christ in them. If our good works are moved *by* the spirit of Christ within us and done *for* the honor of Christ, then it has that acceptable aroma of Christ in it.

D. **High Percentage Yield.**

Nobody outgives God. Those who serve Him with a sincere heart and lovingly relieve the burdens of others may receive back thirty, sixty or a hundredfold, though that should not be the reason. By such incomparable ways, our King rewards our obedience: by unexpected love, by preserving our children, by removing somewhat of that spiritual veil, improved health, by an enhanced joy of our salvation, or satisfaction in our marriage. God knows how to reward our compassion in ways higher or better than we ever thought to ask.

Now we see that charitable, Christ-like good works are a good investment both now and forever. However, it is equally important to see...

II. How Withholding Good Hurts Us.

At some point in the pursuit of happiness, we hit a point of diminishing returns. Trying too hard and spending too much to increase our pleasure can become counter-productive. *"There is a sore evil which I have seen under the sun, namely, riches kept for the owners thereof to their hurt."* (Ecclesiastes 5:13) At some point, keeping too much of our possessions and wealth add more misery than happiness. Adding a private swimming pool or a third house or a fourth car strangely ceases to be pleasurable, and in fact, can diminish the owner's degree of contentedness. It doesn't seem fair. It is a mystery and it is a sore evil. On the brighter side, *"There is (someone) that scatters, and yet increases; and there is he that withholds more than is meet (fair), but it tends to poverty."* (Proverbs 11:24) Many spiritual principles are a paradox. To receive, we must give; heaping up for ourselves commonly results in loss. To truly live, we must in some sense die to ourselves.

III. How Far Should Our Giving Go?

How much am I my brother's keeper? Just how far are we to take our charity? How much do we give and how much do we keep? Where do we draw the line between giving to relieve the miseries of others and indulging more pleasures for ourselves? Will it be niceties for me or necessities for others? (At least, that's how the average American could honestly ask the question.) We will see that the Bible gives us guidelines for this. You probably won't like the answer. I don't. By the way, this chapter does not refer at all to our Christian obligation of tithing. Tithing is not charity; it is obedience. So the question properly put is: how much of my negotiable income, over and above my tithe am I to give?

J. Vernon Magee comments that God notices more what we keep

than what we give. The reason why the widow's two mites impressed Jesus more than the abundant gifts of the rich men was that she kept nothing. *"She of her penury has cast in ALL the living that she had."* (Luke 21:4) This is like the widow who gave to Elijah of her last morsel of bread. For these widows, their giving did not draw on a bank account somewhere, it cost them an immediate physical comfort. They were ready to go hungry.

Remember the lad who donated what was probably his entire lunch of five loaves and two fishes? No doubt, he was ready to go hungry for the honor of presenting it to Jesus. When's the last time you heard of someone sacrificing to the point of physical discomfort or hunger? Satan shrewdly observed, *"Skin for skin, yea, all that a man has will he give for his life"*, that is, for his personal comforts.

The idea is like the old United Way slogan: Give till it hurts. For the disciple of Christ the point is: Give till it costs.

Let's face it, most of our giving today is more casual than costly. Such giving compared to the lad's or the two widows' is like warm embers on the altar compared to red hot coals. I feel like a wimp.

Years ago, I visited the Philippines to meet eight year old Mario Dulay, who was sponsored by World Vision International, a mission organization I supported. It was a delightful trip to the rural village where I finally met Mario and the rest of the family, two parents and eight children. They live on a steep hillside in a two room thatched shack about fifteen feet by twenty feet, just like pictures in *National Geographic.* We had a fascinating time getting acquainted through our interpreter. We were given a royal treatment. The Dulays put together a veritable feast for their guests. We all sat down to eat. It was quite good: home grown vegetables, a tea like drink and roast chicken. Everyone chatted happily over dinner except Mario, who sat across from me. He was visibly downcast and was not eating. His mother and two of the interpreters all urged him to eat. Finally, he nibbled on a few vegetables, but would not touch the chicken. One of them nudged the plate of chicken toward him, but he would not take any. When the interpreter suggested that I try, I nudged the plate toward him and said as kindly as I could, "Try some, Mario." Slowly, his little hand reached toward the plate of chicken. He took a piece and began eating. I expressed my surprise to the others. They explained, "Oh, you're an American; he *can't* refuse you." I really felt lousy. But it was about to get worse. I got to thinking: I never heard of a boy who didn't like chicken, so I asked the interpreter if she knew why Mario had been so reluctant to try the chicken. Mrs. Dulay gave the explanation: the chicken had been his personal pet. That's giving till it costs.

How much each of us should give in a charitable sense may be determined by considering two statements from the Bible. First is the well known quotation of Jesus, "*You shall love your neighbor as yourself.*" The second is found in II Corinthians 8:12-14, "*For if the readiness (willingness) is present, it is acceptable according to what a man has, not according to what he does not have. For this is not for the ease of others and for your affliction, but by way of equality – at this present time your abundance being a supply for their want (shortage), that their abundance also may become a supply for your want, that there may be equality.*"

Notice that acceptable charity is predicated on having the proper disposition about it. It should be motivated by love and such a high degree of love as to be equal to the love we each have for ourselves. Charitable giving should also be done with a ready or willing heart, as opposed to begrudging the gift or resenting the obligation. Next we may deduce that the degree of our obligation is proportional to our possessions or earnings. "*It is acceptable according to what a man has.*" If a person has nothing to spare for giving, but is willing or wishing they could, such a charitable compassion is acceptable to God and to most people. It is surprising that no minimum limit is set for our giving, but rather, that a maximum is given. Evidently, Paul had more concern that the Christians of his time would give too much than too little. The maximum is that they should not give so much to ease others' burdens that they bring affliction upon themselves. How times have changed! Finally, a reasonable guideline is presented for charitable giving, *"that there may be equality."* Rather emphatically, Paul states this twice because he knew their giving would not be easily restrained. They should give no more than what would bring the beneficiaries to a par with themselves. Are they from the same planet as us? Whatever happened to such selfless charity and such genuine love of neighbor? God help us return to it.

"You mean to tell me that God expects me to give away my wealth till everybody around me has the same as me?" You catch on quickly. "But I don't like that idea." Didn't figure you would, since I don't either. But that *is* what He says, like it or not. "But *nobody* does that!" You're right, not lately. But it would sure be nice to see what God would do for the person who did give as this passage says.

Is our faith so shriveled that we try to figure what is the least we can give to God or our neighbor? Why do we recoil at the thought of giving more than our ten percent minimum? It is not just because we are carnal and greedy; mostly, it's because we really don't believe much in God. We believe God will save us and forgive our sins, but we don't believe He would supply our needs and give us joy and a satisfying life. Too many of us relegate God to the religious arena, but when it comes to finances, we tell God, "Access Denied." God must sometimes want to say, "Where do you think all that you have came from in the first place?"

If we would be reasonable, we would see that God has a pretty good track record of reliability. Didn't He prosper undeserving Jacob in all his sojourning? Didn't He provide a table in the wilderness? Didn't He feed faithful Elijah? To this day, *"there has not failed one word of all his good promise."* God give us the grace to trust and obey.

Once we've figured out that we are our brother's keeper, and we are willing to fulfill this duty, there still remains the question...

IV. Where Should My Giving Go?

Since I came to Christ at 21 years old, I have spent nearly an equal amount of time in the pulpit and in the pew. I've sat in the pew and moaned when the topic of the preaching was money. I've also cringed when church finances, or lack thereof, dictated that I say something about it from the pulpit. Allow me to speak in defense of the pastor. Take care of him before anything else. Providing more than comfortably for your pastor is, in my opinion, more important than giving to relieve world hunger. Take care of the man who works hard to take care of you and many others. *"Let the elders that rule well be counted worthy of double honor."* (I Timothy 5:17) Take care of your church and your pastor. That is where your tithe belongs. Never mind that he's not as talented as the evangelist on T.V. That evangelist is not going to be there for you when you're on your back in the hospital or when your teenager runs away and won't listen to you. That evangelist does not pray for you and your family by name day after day, year after year.

As for your giving over and above your tithe, may I suggest six steps in considering what God would want you to do:

Step one: Pray. Ask Him. He is our Counselor. Let's acknowledge Him in all our ways that He may direct our path.

Step two: Study Biblical guidelines. Read the New Testament in particular, looking for answers. For example, *"If any man provide not for his own, and specially for those of his own house, he has denied the faith, and is worse than an infidel."* Caring for our own relatives is clearly a priority. We are also to honor our parents, support the weak, clothe those who lack, feed the hungry, visit the fatherless and widows in their affliction, etc.

Step three: Choose a general direction for your giving. Trust God to lay this on your heart. He knows what is best for the kind of person you are. Yet for a Christian, every option should be linked to the spread of the gospel. Whether our general direction is supporting a local homeless shelter or sending food and medical supplies to Honduras, we should "*do all in the name of the Lord Jesus giving (or causing) thanks unto God and the Father by him.*" (Colossians 3:17)

In some cases, choosing a general direction may result in a life-long commitment, such as supporting a missionary. In other cases, it may be a one-time gift. For example, our church once collected about $500.00 to provide pews for a rural Guatamalan church. Consult your pastor or a good minister with this decision. He's likely to have some appealing ideas and good contacts. Now please don't take the easy way out by having him handle it for you entirely. First, you'll miss out on a lot of fun. Second, your giving would lose a personal element so vital in your praying.

Step four: Choose a general location. You may want to put this step before step three. Location may mean more to you than the type of charity. It does to me. I do as much giving to needs outside the U.S. as I can because the need is so much greater and the effect of one dollar is so much more. For example, ten dollars may feed one homeless person for a day in the U.S., while it would provide about 15 meals in Belize.

"But charity begins at home", someone may object. Not to worry. Charity began at home here a long time ago. But it need not end here.

Some may feel led to provide charitable assistance for only black families, or for AIDS victims, or for orphanages in the Philippines, etc. Generally, whatever most burdens our heart is likely to be where God would have us give. Giving is most effective where prayers from the heart follow. Where our treasure goes, there should our heart be also.

Step five: Fulfill your current obligations. If you are already supporting an elderly aunt or contributing monthly subsistence to a missionary in Mexico, it would seem proper to continue the same level of support for them, rather than think of something more deserving to start supporting. If the giving you are already doing has a scriptural basis and mandate, it's certainly worth continuing. Many excellent missionaries struggling in a difficult area get put out of business because their support from American churches has been shifted to other areas.

However, if your current giving has no direct scriptural basis, and discontinuing support would not cause undue hardship on someone, then it may be more wise to give to a better cause than a lesser. For example, a businessman may make annual contributions to a political party or make regular endowments to a private school. Although the case could be made that such giving is doing some good, there would be little room for argument that transferring that support to a church planter in Malaysia would be more profitable to the kingdom of God. In the first case, the political party might reward you; in the second case, God himself would certainly reward you.

Step six: Tighten the belt. In our debt-laden society, we have a terrible habit of borrowing to the hilt. We treat our bank balances like we do speed limits. We drive as if "Speed Limit 50" means "don't go slower than 50." Likewise, if our bank account looks like it's even thinking about getting above zero, we feel obligated to hurry out to buy something.

This step is not easy. But for a lot of us, increasing our giving will necessitate a major adjustment to our living standard. If we've already "maxed" out our monthly spending with a thousand dollar house note, a five hundred dollar car note, and sundry other monthly bills and notes, then it's easy for our charitable giving to become strained. If we're loading up our mortgages and credit cards to keep ourselves *"clothed in purple and fine linen and faring sumptuously every day"*, we won't have much to spare for Lazarus. Obviously, the time to deal with this problem is *before* we make the purchases. We have to be willing to spend less on ourselves or on our families if we want to be in a posture to do more giving.

There are Christian families who have come to this realization and sold their homes and high priced vehicles, and bought more modestly priced ones instead. Others may achieve the same financial liberty by re-financing, by simplifying vacation plans, canceling club memberships, subscriptions, etc.

The motivation for such commendable sacrifices should be:

a. **Love for the Lord Jesus.** Wanting to promote his interest and honor in this world. To live out our own prayer *"thy kingdom come"*. We want to assist in the support of the gospel of Christ, which *"is the power of God unto salvation to every one that believes."*
b. **Love for our neighbor.** I wish every American (especially teenagers) would visit the slums of Tijuana, Mexico, the boat city of Hong Kong, and see the poverty of the rural regions around the world. This is the world that God so loves, and so should we. Jesus came into this world to give his life a ransom for many. Would not making modest sacrifices for our neighbor be but reasonable service?
c. **For the joy of it.** We may have Christmas year round, if we give for the happiness and relief of others year round. This sort of joy is a little earnest of heaven and is bequeathed to us in this life. *"These things have I spoken unto you, that my joy might remain in you, and that your joy might be full."* (John 15:11) We may expect to share in God's joy when we share in His work.

V. Leave Room for the Unexpected.

We should *"be ready to every good work"*, and keep ourselves in a position *"to do good unto all men"* as we find opportunity. It seems that God sends opportunities our way from time to time. It may be a stranded motorist, a homeless person or family, or a plea for help with someone's power bill. Being *"ready to every good work"* would be keeping in a frame of mind to be cheerfully willing to do good at every opportunity. Let's follow the example of Abraham, who saw three strangers passing through and *"ran to meet them"* saying, *"Let a little water be fetched and wash your feet and rest yourselves under the tree, and I will fetch a morsel of bread... and Abraham hastened into the tent"* to cook a dinner for them. (Genesis 18:2-6)

Consider also the hospitality of Rebecca, who upon seeing a group of travelers come to town, *"she hasted and let down her pitcher...and gave him drink."* She also drew water for a number of camels and then invited the entire caravan to spend the night at her father's home.

Then there was Barzillai, a wealthy man, who at the risk of his life, delivered a vast supply of food and goods to David and his family when they fled from Absalom. In contrast was the desperately poor widow of Zarephath who fed Elijah with her last morsel of food.

It is probable that none of these performed their kindnesses with any thought of reward. Rather they simply enjoyed doing good, made it a lifestyle and kept themselves ready for the unexpected.

In conclusion, let's look for opportunities God brings our way. It may involve sending a financial gift to the other side of the planet or it may require that we roll our own sleeves up and get busy. Whether we entertain angels in the process or not, let's be eager to do good to all men, for this would be well-pleasing to Him.

"Beloved, I wish above all things that you may prosper and be in health."

III John 2

Does God Want Me to be Healthy?

I. Does God Want Me to Be Healthy?

Obviously, God would not want us to be negligent in the care of our health. Since our bodies are the temple of the Holy Spirit, we ought to take care of them. Without doting upon ourselves, we should practice normal hygiene and exercise reasonable prudence in staying healthy. We'd be a lot more useful in service to God and man in good health, than laid up in a hospital with pneumonia.

But aside from suffering as a result of foolishly hazarding our health, is it possible that God would ever want me to suffer, or hurt, or grieve, or have pain or loss? As was said in the opening lines of this book, of course it is God's will that we be in good health. God takes no pleasure in our sufferings, heartbreaks, disabilities, etc. In fact, our heavenly Father, in His kindness, originally planned for all of creation to have no suffering, grief or even death. God created man to enjoy paradise on earth with Him, and for a while, that's exactly what happened. The good news is that God is now forging a future for us that again includes perfect bliss, free from any kind of suffering. *"And God shall wipe away all tears from their eyes; and there shall be no more death, neither sorrow, nor crying, neither shall there be any more pain: for the former things are passed away."*

(Revelation 21:4) In the meantime, *"these former things"* seem to be an integral and necessary part of life. The question is: "Why?"

We have further indication that in present times, God makes extensive provision to alleviate or eliminate sufferings. It is God who inspires man toward developments in the medical field and puts it in the hearts of some to be nurses, doctors, etc. So on the one side, He makes doctors and nurses His right and left hand of ministering to the hurting, while on the other side, such vocations tend to draw out compassion and love from those doing the ministering. So God works good at both ends. Without need, there could be no opportunity to give; nor could there be gratitude for needs fulfilled.

God also provided the church with men (and women) gifted to do miraculous healings. *"But the manifestation of the Spirit is given to every man to profit withal...to another, the gifts of healing by the same Spirit."* (I Corinthians 12:7,9) Many Christians believe that God can and does heal today. But some make the mistake of relegating the *gift* of healing to apostolic times. The gift is as real and as valid today as ever. Too much theological cold water has been thrown on the faith of those who might otherwise believe in spiritual gifts for today and learn to use them. When people are told that such spiritual gifts are not for today, it becomes a self-fulfilling prophecy for them. The truth is: real, miraculous healing is indeed occurring today. Unfortunately, in some circles, where skepticism appears, the same problem arises that Jesus found in his own country, *"And he could there do no mighty work, save that he laid his hands upon a few sick folk, and healed them."* (Mark 6:5)

Too much theological cold water has been thrown on the faith of those who might otherwise believe in spiritual gifts for today and learn to use them.

In other circles, where faith in spiritual gifts is cultivated, greater healings are occurring, some phonies notwithstanding. It has always been the case that it shall be unto us according to our faith.

Getting back to the question: "Does God want me to be healthy", we may conclude that when we see how much provision He has made for our good health and comfort, that the answer is "yes".

II. So why is there so much suffering in the world?

We'd be pretty safe in blaming ourselves for a big part of it. Man's inhumanity to man has caused untold suffering in countless wars, brutal regimes, etc. Man's neglect of morality has resulted in sexually transmitted diseases. Selfishness has broken many homes and hearts. Man's neglect of his own health accounts for the majority of cancer, diabetes, heart disease, etc. Yet there are those who blame God for all this, mainly because He could stop all the suffering and heal all the sick if He chose.

We now face a serious dilemma: in both the medical field and in the matter of praying for the sick, why are some healed and others not? Why doesn't God heal them all? There's an answer. In both the natural and the spiritual world, we are subject to God-ordained laws. In the natural world, if we combine a combustible material with oxygen and provide a spark, combustion occurs every time. (Except when it's your car and you're late for work.)

Likewise in the spiritual world, God has laws governing how spiritual "combustion" (or healing) occurs. Scripture gives clear criteria that must be fulfilled concurrently. Typically, Christians, even those who believe in the healing power of God, do not follow Biblical directions. As combustion must have all three of the ingredients, oxygen, a spark and combustible material, so all the elements required by Scripture must be present for healing to occur. James 5:16 lists some of them: *"Confess your faults one to another, and pray for one another, that you may be healed. The effectual, fervent prayer of a righteous man avails much."* Having plenty of spark and combustible material can never make up for lack of oxygen. All three must be present. Similarly, having ample righteousness and faith will do no good if effectual, fervent prayer does not also occur.

Notice the verse begins with a call to humility: ***"Confess your faults one to another."*** *"Faults"* may apply to bodily or spiritual deficiencies. Either way, it is as humbling to admit when one has infected sinuses, as it is to confess a problem with lust. Confessing our sins as well as our maladies sets the stage for peace with God and improves the likelihood of a healing. Note that we are not called to confess everybody else's faults one to another, which is a lot more popular. We are to confess our own. The instructions also do not read that just the sick shall confess his faults to the elders. Rather, everyone should do some confessing to the others. If the elders have come ready to anoint the sick with oil, it would be a good preparation for them to confess as well. *"For all have sinned and have come short of the glory of God."* (Romans 3:23) If this step is bypassed, we have less reason to believe healing will occur. This step would be like making sure all the air and fuel ports and spark plugs of an engine are clean, so that the power can flow.

We are not called upon to confess everybody else's faults one to another, which is a lot more popular.

The next step is ***"pray for one another."*** This is God's invitation to call on Him in our times of need. We are to ask if we wish to receive. When the blind man of Jericho heard that Jesus of Nazareth passes by, he was brought to stand face to face with Jesus. Although it could not have been more obvious that the man was blind and that his aching desire was to be able to see, yet Jesus asked him the question, *"What will you* *that I should do unto you?"* I used to wonder why the blind man didn't say, "What do you think I want? You can see very well I'm blind." But he very politely answered, *"Lord, that I may receive my sight."* Upon his asking, Jesus immediately heals him, explaining, *"Your faith has saved you."* (Luke 18:36-43)

"Well if God already knows what I need before I ask, there's no need to actually ask, right?" Yes, He knows, but He wants us to ask. Idly waiting for God to heal us is a bit presumptuous, but asking is faith. And God always rewards faith.

So we are to prepare with confession and then pray *"for one another."* While our confession is to focus largely on ourselves, our praying should focus largely on others. How much better it is for one child of God to pray lovingly for another, than for all of us to pray only for ourselves.

Notice now how the atmosphere is congealing for this healing service: humility, confession, compassion toward one another's needs and praying unselfishly for one another. Things are heating up. Conditions for "combustion" are coming together.

Right in the middle of this verse, we see the whole point of the verse: ***"that you may be healed."*** Let us fasten our faith upon this phrase, as men of old laid hold of the horns of the altar. Let us learn to pray, "Lord, we've done all we know to do; we've confessed our faults, and we're praying for our hurting brother here. Now God, make good your word to us, *"that he may be healed."* That's good preparation and good praying. However, there's more.

Next, we see who is to be in attendance at this meeting: ***"a righteous man."*** When Jesus went to raise Jairus' daughter, all the unbelieving guests were put out before the "healing service" began. When believers or elders are called on to go pray for the healing of the sick, let me suggest that nobody else come. Only righteous saints who also believe in miraculous healing should be present. I recommend against someone coming along just for the ride or for the experience. When surgeons go to the operating room, there are no spectators or loiterers allowed. The last thing we need when we're trying to achieve spiritual "combustion" is somebody to quench the Spirit.

The praying man must be in good standing with God. Fervent praying does not avail if the man is not righteous. Claiming even the authority of Christ would be futile, as the seven sons of Sceva found out. (Acts 19:13-16) He must have the righteousness of God, not just his own righteousness. He continuously bears good fruit and his fruit remains, so that whatever he asks of the Father in Christ's name, He will give it to him. He does not stop his ears at the cry of the poor; he gives himself to the hungry and satisfies the desire of the afflicted. He has done all this good and served God and put his shoulder to the plow. If this man has received little acknowledgement or compensation for the good he has done, all the better, for he would have significant treasure in heaven. But this righteous man thinks little enough of himself or his labor so that he never boasts of it before men (as Godly Mordecai, who never mentioned that he had saved the emperor's life). He does not even mention his good before God, as the self-righteous Pharisee. Thus, this righteous man's treasure remains intact. God will surely hear this man. *"The eyes of the Lord are upon the righteous, and his ears are open unto their cry."* (Psalm 34:15) His prayers and alms go up for a memorial before God.

Not only must there be righteous men (or women) present, but the praying must be ***"effectual"*** and ***"fervent"***. The righteous man must pray with intensity and determination, not necessarily with volume, show or gesticulation. He prays with faith, believing that God can be imposed upon to grant the petition. Though the case seems hard, the heavens closed and God obstinate, yet he persists in prevailing, pushy prayer, as:

a. the woman who hounded the unjust judge;

b. Jacob, who would not let go until he obtained the blessing;
c. the woman from the coasts of Tyre who prevailed over the seeming refusals of Jesus; (Mark 7:24-30)
d. the persistent man who knocked on his friend's door at night needing three loaves of bread. (Luke 11:5)

This is effectual praying. Effectual prayer is forging ahead, pressing to the throne, ascending into heavenly places, losing all sense of surrounding or self-consciousness, staying fixed and focused on pleading the case before Him, single-mindedly oblivious of all else.

> *Effectual prayer is forging ahead, pressing to the throne, ascending into heavenly places, losing all sense of surrounding or self-consciousness, staying fixed and focused on pleading the case before Him, single-mindedly oblivious of all else.*

I have the feeling that too much of our praying today is lamely casual and leisurely, rather than effectual and fervent. How rare are the occasions that our prayer is travailing and prevailing. We don't pray hard enough, long enough, often enough or serious enough. How do we thus raise the temperature on our altar of incense, so that our praying is fervent and hot, as the glowing coals? By having inflamed desire, as Rachel's impassioned, "*Give me children, or else I die!*" To intensify our prayer for the sick, we may "*remember them which suffer adversity as being (ourselves) also in the body.*" (Hebrews 13:3) How much more effective our praying becomes when we project ourselves into others, feeling their miseries, hurting with them, approaching their same desire to have relief. Mothers are good at this.

To review, we now have a prayer gathering at the bedside of an ailing brother. We find an atmosphere of humility and confession. Righteous men have gathered – and only righteous men. Effectual, fervent prayer has ascended before the throne of God. There is anticipation and expectation of miraculous healing because the righteous man believes his praying ***"avails much"*** since God said so.

In many cases, healing is enacted at this point. Sometimes the healing is immediate and dramatic. At other times, the healing begins when the prayer is made and the improvement progresses over a period of time. In yet other instances, healing does not occur. Though the righteous man prays effectually and fervently, sometimes he avails and sometimes he fails. That's what happened to Elijah. Remember the well-to-do couple whose little boy died abruptly? (I Kings 17:17ff) Righteous Elijah was invited to come pray. We can be sure that nothing but effectual, fervent prayer issued from his mouth, for the record says twice, *"and he cried unto the Lord."* Guess what happened when righteous, mighty Elijah prayed effectually and fervently that God would restore the little boy back to life? Nothing. That's right. God flat turned him down. Elijah could easily have said, "Well, Mrs. Smith, sometimes it's not God's will to heal someone." Instead, he cried unto the Lord again, praying with much earnest and desire and compassion, pouring out his soul in requesting the life of the child. Now guess what happened? Nothing. God turned him down again. But Elijah wouldn't quit. He was just like you and me, except that he wouldn't quit. He persisted with God and got his way the third time and life came back into the little boy's body. We get annoyed when our children ask us two and three times for the same thing. "That's enough", we'll chide, "Don't bring it up to me again." But we must not think God is so.

How about the time when Elijah prayed for rain? Remember, faithful Elijah had put his life on the line as King Ahab led a world wide man hunt to find him. And it was Elijah at Mt. Carmel who almost single-handedly turned the heart of Israel back to the Lord their God. This could easily have resulted in the loss of his life, too. Faithful Elijah. How could God turn him down when he prayed for rain for his nation? But God did. God did not send rain. Then while Ahab feasted and Elijah fasted and prayed a second time for rain, God refused him again and then again. Yet Elijah prayed seven times before God finally sent the rain he had been asking for. So the lesson is: don't quit.

When you know your car has gas, you know the engine is getting air and a good spark, but it doesn't crank the first time, what do you do? You turn the key again and again. Most folks would probably try a dozen times before giving up. So with far more at stake, why should we give up praying after a couple of tries? However, if the car doesn't start or if the prayer is not granted after a few attempts, it may be time to stop and do an assessment.

At one point when David was king, Israel suffered a devastating three year famine. No doubt, David and a lot of his people had been praying for rain, but to no avail. Something was wrong. Their prayers weren't working. So David did some assessment. He *"enquired of the Lord."* (II Samuel 21:1) God answered David and explained, *"It is for Saul and for his bloody house, because he slew the Gibeonites."* In other words, Israel had sinned collectively against the Gibeonites years ago and had never repented and made amends. David and Israel made reparation with the people of Gibeon. Then God granted their prayers and the famine ended.

If our prayers are repeatedly denied, we also need to find out why and make right whatever is wrong. Husbands are cautioned to *"give honor unto the wife as unto the weaker vessel, and as being heirs together of the grace of life; that your prayers be not hindered."* (I Peter 3:7) Sometimes our prayer service to heal the sick is all systems go, yet repeated efforts have been to no avail. We have done some honest personal assessment and turned up nothing. Why is it that, even then, when everything looks right, still our requests are declined?

III. There Are Times When It Is God's Will That Someone Suffer.

Let me first make this clear: I am not saying God is pleased to see anyone suffer just for the sufferings' sake. God is so far from being like cruel children who will torture some little creature just for the sadistic pleasure of it. Rather, we find ample Biblical support for the idea that God permits and ordains sufferings and afflictions even for His children – especially for His children, but for their good. *"It is good for me that I have been afflicted; that I might learn thy statutes."* (Psalm 119:71)

We may divide the cases in which God allows human suffering into three categories:

a. Punitive
b. Corrective
c. Instructive

Punitive would be suffering applied to unbelievers who are yet in their sins and must bear the full penalty of retribution for all their misdeeds. Those are more fortunate, who in this life fall into the hands of the living God, than those who continue in their sin, have an easy time of it in this life but must later suffer eternal judgment. (Hebrews 10:31) When God makes the way of the sinner hard in this life, it is a mercy to them. (Proverbs 13:15) They are more likely to see the error of their ways and turn back from disobedience. It was God's mercy to Pharaoh that He withstood him and his army in the pillar of fire and hindered them as they stubbornly pressed on in pursuit of Israel. God mercifully tried to stop him. By the way, Pharaoh was the last man on earth to deserve such a merciful warning. What mercy or patience did Pharaoh deserve who slaughtered more infant boys than Herod ever thought about? This is the man who also led a brutal regime, severely oppressing the honest Hebrew people.

The Bible tells us that the Lord *"troubled the host of the Egyptians, and took off their chariot wheels, that they drove them heavily."* (Exodus 14:24,25) The Egyptians got the message all right. On perceiving that the hand of God was against them, they said among themselves, *"Let us flee from the face of Israel; for the Lord fights for them against the Egyptians."* Pharaoh and his army ignored God's warnings and soon after, tragically, but justly, drowned in the Red Sea. How often does our kind God send similar warnings to dishonest men today. May they fare better than Pharaoh.

God sends punitive suffering to some today. This is often the natural result of a man's lifestyle. The heavy drinker develops health problems and dies at a young age. The smoker gets heart disease and lung cancer. Others develop overweight conditions from poor eating habits. God might use any kind of pain, loss or tragedy as punitive action to warn a sinner. When God ordains such things for this life, it is surely in hopes of saving someone from eternal judgment.

Corrective suffering is very much like punitive, except that corrective measures are administered only to a child of God for their instruction and improvement when they have sinned. *"Whom the Lord loves he chastens, and scourges every son whom he receives."* (Hebrews 12:6) God takes vengeance on the wicked, but *"God has not appointed us to wrath."* That is, God deals more as a father toward his adopted children. He cherishes each one tenderly and affectionately. All His dealings with His child are for the child's good. The chastening that is administered is done in merciful kindness, so that He will not let His child be tempted above what he can bear. This does not mean that God is lenient or lax in dealing with His child's sin. Quite to the contrary, we can be sure God holds us to a higher standard than others. So the child of God may more surely expect the chastising hand of God than the outsider. Being a Christian does not exempt anybody from suffering.

Being a Christian does not exempt anybody from suffering.

Biblical accounts tell that in extreme cases of rebellion, God was willing to send troubles and diseases on His people to turn them from their sins. He warned them that He would. If they would not obey Him, this would be the consequence: *"I will bring a sword upon you, that shall avenge the quarrel of my covenant: and when you are gathered within your cities, I will send the pestilence among you."* (Leviticus 26:25) God did so later in the terrible sieges of Israel, but only to bring His covenant people to their knees in repentance. So sometimes God allows suffering even to his children, in order to correct or improve them.

Instructive. God's will for each of us is our sanctification, our maturing in the spirit and developing into the fullness of the stature of Jesus Christ. Anyone who has reared children understands the complexity of the process. Sometimes sound instruction instills the principle or character needed, sometimes repetition, sometimes forcefulness, sometimes a gentle plea and sometimes pain is necessary. So many growing pains of childhood are a vital and valuable experience for us whether it's struggling with school, agonizing over love rejected, enduring the pain of hard workouts, measles, flu, or even punish work or spankings. Every one of these childhood sufferings works an obvious benefit for the maturing child. Struggling through school prepares a child for the rigors of the professional world; emotional heartbreak seasons their compassion and increases their ability to love probably more than the happier relationships. Grueling workouts and hard running condition a young man to win championships and help him develop a healthy, competitive spirit. Bouts with the measles and flu immunize him against future sicknesses, while punish work and spankings train him to be honest, obedient and kind. Which of these sufferings would we remove from the child's life? "Sparing" him from any one of these would result in the child later being deficient in some way as an adult. His development would suffer. A parent who would remove any of these constructive sufferings of life would be acting unwisely, and actually depriving their child of needed qualities. Still though, a parent loves their child, hates to see their child suffer, indeed suffers with their child, and would take the pain for their child if they could.

Most any parent understands these simple truths because they've been through it and it's obvious to them. However, what might not be so clear is that this is the position God is in. He loves His children, too. He would take the pain for His child too (and He has). Yet if He were to spare His child from *all* suffering, the child would be under-developed and handicapped. He would fall far short of the potential God designed for him. So why does God allow suffering for the believer?

IV. How Does Suffering Benefit the Christian?

Suffering, in general, puts such an intangible quality in the soul that cannot be achieved any other way. Such a serene, heavenly glow of love, maturity and selflessness emanate from the face of a woman who has just suffered through hours of labor pains. "*Notwithstanding, she shall be saved in child-bearing.*" (I Timothy 2:15) That is, the woman's suffering in labor pains has a wholesome, sanctifying effect on her, which fits her for heavenly service. God allows this and ordains this for her good. He accomplishes this refinement of her soul just in time to put self in a secondary position in order to give all necessary attention and care to a newborn infant.

Similarly, bad health, affliction and any kind of suffering have a way of purging or immunizing us against sin. "*Forasmuch then as Christ has suffered for us in the flesh, arm yourselves likewise with the same mind: for he that has suffered in the flesh had ceased from sin; that he no longer should live the rest of his time in the flesh to the lusts of men, but to the will of God."* (I Peter 4:1,2)

Notice the clause: "*he that has suffered in the flesh has ceased from sin.*" This most certainly does *not* refer to Christ, mentioned earlier in the verse, for Christ never began to sin, and therefore could never cease to sin. Rather, this golden truth may be applied to any man, especially, I would think, to a Christian. Bodily suffering and pain have the very desirable effect of diminishing the power of sin in us.

Bodily suffering and pain have the very desirable effect of diminishing the power of sin in us.

That part of self in us that has such an appetite for sin is dealt a damaging blow. Sin suffers a loss in its attempt to reign in our mortal body. The greater the suffering, the more the old man of sin is crucified. After a season of grief, hardship, deprivation or pain, the saint comes through stronger, wiser and more able to defeat sin. He lives no longer so much for the lusts of men, but for the will of God. Why does God allow suffering in His child? To help him put to death the old nature of sin and give prevalence to the new nature, the new creation in him. For that must increase and the old must decrease.

V. Why does God allow suffering in the Christian?

There was a great deal of suffering in the days of the apostles when the New Testament was written. Consequently, the subject got a lot of attention in their writings. The people suffered; the apostles suffered. They went through sickness, endured persecution, beatings, imprisonments, suffered disabilities, bereavements, heartbreaks, poverty – much like today. It was revealed to Peter by the Holy Spirit, that in all these trials there was design.

God intends to refine the gold of our Christian character. ***"Wherein you greatly rejoice, though now for a season, if need be, you are in heaviness through manifold temptations: that the trial of your faith, being much more precious than of gold that perishes, though it be tried with fire, might be found unto praise and honor and glory at the appearing of Jesus Christ."*** (I Peter 1:6,7)

Try to hang on to the complex phraseology of this passage; the priceless truths here are well worth grasping. Under the inspiration of the Holy Spirit, Peter begins by saying we have reason to greatly rejoice over what he is about to reveal.

God gives us good news: Temptations (trials) are but "***for a season***", not forever, as it may seem when in the midst of them. "Oh, God, when will this end?" "How long, O Lord", we cry. Yet "*weeping endures but for a night, but joy comes in the morning.*" (Psalm 30:5) Our light affliction is but for a moment. All the pain, sufferings and anguishes of this life shall seem so short when we look back on them in the world to come. Our reward on high by comparison shall seem to be a "*far more exceeding and eternal weight of glory.*" (II Corinthians 4:17) What marathon winner basking in the glory of his victory regrets the torture his legs and lungs endured? What mother joyously cradling her new born infant counts the pains she endured in childbirth worthy to be compared with the treasure they resulted in? Suffering, especially for Christ's sake, is a real bargain. We benefit far more than we suffer.

Yes, God allows suffering, weeping and temptation, but He carefully prescribes it in manageable degrees. He will not let us be over-burdened with suffering in either intensity or longevity. "*God is faithful, who will not suffer you to be tempted above that you are able.*" No beloved child of God can say, as murderous Cain, "*My punishment is greater than I can bear.*" Even so, God was merciful enough even to him. How much more shall the tender mercies of our good Father be with His child.

The next words of this verse are very telling: "***if need be.***" There are times when the shortfalls of our maturing and character need the refining, strengthening effect of suffering or affliction. There are also vital lessons to be learned and qualities to be acquired that easy, comfortable living cannot produce. In regard to suffering, we're never glad it comes, but should be glad it came. "*No chastening for the present seems to be joyous.*" It is usually later that we come to realize the benefit. "*Afterward it yields the peaceable fruit of righteousness.*" (Hebrews 12:11)

Suffering: we're never glad it comes, but should be glad it came.

"*If need be*", and when it needs be. God designs, schedules and orchestrates all the trials of life. His wisdom will allow no less than need be and His sovereignty will allow no more. There shall no strange thing happen to any of God's own that He is not aware of and that He does not approve of. "*Beloved, think it not strange concerning the fiery trial which is to try you, as though some strange thing happened unto you.*" (I Peter 4:12) He is ever aware of our state, has His finger on our pulse and His hand upon our brow, ensuring that we're not pushed beyond our limit. He never leaves us or forsakes us especially when we walk through the valley of the shadow of death. He is with us always, even to the end of the world. Let this be our sweet consolation in sorrowful times. If suffering or pain be needful for our soul, we can be sure that the Friend who sticks closer than a brother will be with us through it all. "*For we have not a high priest which cannot be touched with the feeling of our infirmities; but was in all points tempted like as we are.*" (Hebrews 4:15)

Thus our friend, Jesus, is intently aware that we "***are in heaviness***

***through manifold temptations.*"** He knows the heaviness of His blessed ones who suffer, being bed-ridden, or crippled with arthritis, or battling with cancer. He is acutely aware of all that we are enduring. Those who embrace Him in their trials, He shall give them, "*the garment of praise for the spirit of heaviness.*" (Isaiah 61:3) He will give them rejoicing and reason to rejoice.

In verse seven, we find the meat of the message. The first word, "***that***", links verses six and seven and indicates that what follows is the reason for what precedes. What precedes is the fact that we must suffer manifold temptations. The words following in verse seven explain why this must be.

First, "***the trial of your faith.***" Why does God allow the Christian to suffer? To try, refine, prove and demonstrate his faith, steadfastness, trust and character. In other words, in addition to God's perfecting his qualities, He's also showing him off, proudly displaying him, as God did with Job. "*Hast thou considered my servant Job?*" The trying of our faith is necessary to the developing of our faith. How necessary, how important, how valuable to us is the trial of our faith?

It is "***more precious than gold.***" David was a better man after God passed him through the fiery trials of false accusation, persecution, attempts on his life, separation, deprivation, loss and illness. The raw gold of his character must become fine gold of Ophir if he is to be king. Likewise must God refine the gold of every believer who has committed their soul into His care. He has a destiny set for each one, and He will not be negligent in their preparation and cultivation. The only gold that is put through the fire is that which is intended for some noble use. Maybe a medallion, maybe jewelry to adorn a queen. Are you being put through the fire? Congratulations. Great things await you.

We see choice men of God in the Bible, far from being exempt from hardship, being put through much more than their share. Joseph suffered more than all his brothers and rose to greatness. David did likewise, as well as Elijah, and John the Baptist, and the apostles. More contemporary examples could be listed by the hundreds: C.T. Studd, George Washington, Adoniram Judson, etc.

So often do we see suffering and hardship or sickness as part of God's venue for preparing a man for greatness, that when we do see these in a man's life, we come to almost expect the person to rise to greatness.

What Is Greatness? Greatness must not be confused with prominence. No character or virtue is needed to be prominent, famous, popular or to be in a position of power or influence. Greatness is not in holding high political or corporate office; greatness is not in fame or in the acquisition of wealth; greatness is not in winning beauty pageants or athletic contests.

True greatness begins when a man has conquered himself, when he is crucified with Christ, when he has denied himself and subdued lust, greed and self-centeredness.

True greatness begins when a man has conquered himself, when he is crucified with Christ, when he has denied himself and subdued lust, greed and self-centeredness.

True greatness is achieved when a man ceases to love and serve himself and he begins to live for the sake and for the good of others. He expends himself in promoting, bettering and nurturing others, quite forgetful of himself. The sole preoccupation of his mind is to see how much good for others he can do each day. True greatness is attained when such a man conveys not only his service, but his very soul to people around him. He becomes good leaven affecting the whole lump. Many pastors and missionaries are truly great men, though rarely recognized as such. Jesus was such a great man, as well as John the Baptist, Paul and Barnabas. These were both great and prominent, but they were not great *because* they were prominent. Many to whom the world ascribes greatness, are little more than famous or talented. So often it is the case: *"that which is highly esteemed among men is abomination in the sight of God."* (Luke 16:15)

The next words put an even greater value on the trying of our faith: ***"that perishes."*** The transitory nature of the wealth or gold of this world certainly de-values it. It is presented in contrast with the precious, priceless value of faith fully developed. Gold may be spent only one time on a purchase, while our faith reaps us daily dividends to eternity. Faith is an eternal value well worth cultivating. *"And now abides faith, hope, charity (love), these three; but the greatest of these is charity (love)."* (I Corinthians 13:13)

Our rich text continues: ***"though it be tried by fire."*** Here the text very aptly compares the refining process of gold with the trial of our faith. Natural gold is not very impressive in appearance. It has very little luster to it because of the impurities in it. Sometimes the only way to tell that a rock or nugget has gold in it is by its exceptionally heavy weight. Gold is nearly as heavy as lead. This is like a fledgling Christian: not particularly impressive in conduct at first, but there is something inside of extremely high value – the indwelling Holy Spirit. Gold, in its natural form, would not be of much value or use. However, the nice thing about raw gold is that it has tremendous potential value. Again this is like the new Christian who is inexperienced and of limited usefulness to God's purposes, but has unlimited potential. For God, through him, is *"able to do exceeding abundantly above all that we ask or think according to the power that works in us."* (Ephesians 3:20) Now God holds this weighty gold nugget in His hand that is unlimited in value and potential – you! Your Master designs to refine and perfect you, to purify you and elevate you to your fullest value. *"For we are his workmanship."* (Ephesians 2:10)

The metallurgist who plans to perfect his gold understands that there is only so much that can be done to enhance the gold's appearance or usefulness. He might get a chisel and chip away chunks of other minerals the gold is imbedded in. This would be like a new Christian separating himself from sinful or ungodly relationships. That helps.

Next the metallurgist might try to sand and polish what gold may be showing. This would be a fairly useless exercise and would correspond to a Christian polishing only the outward appearance, but making no real internal change. This is making clean the outside of the cup and platter, while within being full of extortion and excess. (Matthew 23:25) This is the Christian who makes his appearances at church, dresses attractively, has a pleasant charming manner, but has never discarded worldly values and sought the filling of the Holy Spirit. His Christianity is all on the surface, rather than assimilated into the core of his being. He'll turn out for the church softball games, but decline to take part in prayer meetings. He's honest and sincere, but spiritually lethargic and impotent. The well-structured sermons he hears weekly are just not making an impact on him. He tries to be dutiful in his Bible reading and praying, but the verses seem so flat and his prayers seem so feeble. He knows he should love his neighbor as himself and he tries genuinely to love people more. Yet he feels like he's trying to conjure something up in his heart that just isn't there. He is frustrated that his Christian development seems to have stalled and he's getting nowhere. What can he do? The answer is in Revelation 3:18, *"I counsel thee to buy of me gold tried in the fire."*

What happens is that a Christian develops and matures only so far in comfortable, easy times. But if further progress is to be made, somebody's got to turn the heat up. Once the raw gold is put into a smelting pot and the temperature is raised a couple of thousand degrees, an interesting phenomenon begins to occur. The whole rock consisting of mineral and gold mixture melts down and laminates. That is, it separates out into different layers, the heavier gold settling to the bottom and the lighter minerals floating to the top. At this point, the mineral can be brushed off the surface of the liquid gold, leaving nothing but pure gold.

In some inexplicable way, the same thing happens to a Christian when God puts them through a fiery trial. Somehow the affliction, pain or anguish has a way of burning off or purging out deeply imbedded character defects, subduing self-centeredness and crucifying the sin nature. When such dross is purged out and only golden qualities remain, a new man emerges. Miraculously, the man becomes tenderhearted as never before, his love and closeness to God rise to a higher plane, and he cares about people as never before. Sometimes, God is willing to let us forfeit what we cannot keep to gain what we cannot lose.

Sometimes, God is willing to let us forfeit what we cannot keep to gain what we cannot lose.

If we saw the long view of things that God does, we'd be *asking* Him to put us through the purifying fire, rather than begging desperately to be taken out of it. When our faith, love, body or soul is tried or tempered with the fire of suffering, we will always be great gainers through it.

Last of all, we see the intended outcome of having been put through the fire: that you (your faith) ***"might be found unto praise and honor and glory at the appearing of Jesus Christ."*** Just as Christ suffered first and then entered into his glory, so *"if we suffer, we shall also reign with him."* (II Timothy 2:12) We also are called to be *"partakers of the afflictions of the gospel."* Those who are partakers of the sufferings shall also be partakers of the consolation. (II Corinthians 1:7) If we find ourselves privileged to do so, there shall surely be great reward according to the promise: *"Blessed are you when men shall revile you, persecute you, and shall say all manner of evil against you falsely, for my sake. Rejoice and be exceedingly glad: for great is your reward in heaven."* (Matthew 5:12) Likewise for those who live Godly and yet suffer bad health, grief, bankruptcy, etc. God has rewards for all His soldiers who suffer in the line of duty.

Suffering, pain or poor health is a privilege and a high honor put upon some of God's choice children. They are called upon, as Paul, to *"fill up that which is behind of the afflictions of Christ...for his body's sake, which is the church."* (Colossians 1:24) As the blood of the martyrs was the seed of the church, so the suffering of the saints is the nurture of the church. The suffering of one church member benefits not only himself, but the church at large in some mystical way. There is a ministry of suffering. It seems to me that the suffering of a Christian increases the gold reserves of the church. The suffering Christian feels useless if they are not doing anything constructive for others. They may be bedridden and not even able to pray. Yet consider that the economy of an entire nation is founded on its gold reserves. Remove the gold and the currency becomes worthless. Yet the gold just sits there, doing nothing. Its value does not consist in what it does, but in its inherent worth. Gold is worth something because it has been through the fire. Likewise for God's saint. Let every wheelchair bound believer and all our elderly who are worn out from a lifetime of good works and from laboring in love be treated with every honor and care, for without the vast reserves of their worth and former works, the net spiritual worth our churches would suffer heavy losses.

Why does God allow us to suffer? That we may shine brighter for Him in this dark world. Of John the Baptist, Jesus declared, *"He was a burning and a shining light: and you were willing for a season to rejoice in his light."* (John 5:35) He shone with the gifts and graces of God. What a joy it must have been to him to be so eminently useful to God in serving his generation. But John was a *burning* and shining light. He was a shining light only because he was first a burning light. As a child, he was separated from his family unto the Lord, as Samuel. Far from the comforts of community living, he lived solitary in the wilderness, as Moses and Elijah, *"till the day of his showing unto Israel."* He suffered deprivation, exposure and hunger. He fasted, kept no luxuries, had no house and ate locusts and wild honey. Later, he suffered ridicule, persecution, imprisonment and death. He was hated for righteousness' sake. Yes, John was a *burning* and shining light.

We all want to shine, but nobody wants to burn. However, every light that shines must also burn. But what an honor it is! The great Bible commentator, Matthew Henry, writes, "To suffer for the sake of Christ is a valuable gift… it is a great honor and a great advantage; for we may be very serviceable to the glory of God." (Matthew Henry Commentary, vol. 6, pg. 730)

"To suffer for the sake of Christ is a valuable gift…
it is a great honor and a great advantage; for we
may be very serviceable to the glory of God."
(Matthew Henry)

"For unto you it is given in the behalf of Christ, not only to believe on him, but also to suffer for his sake." (Philippians 1:29)

Does God want me to be healthy? Absolutely. But He values our spiritual fitness more than our physical. If, in His wisdom, our sovereign Master deems it best that we do without bodily health or comforts for a season, it is for us to say as Job did, *"Though he slay me, yet will I trust in him."* Sometimes we must say, "It's been rough with my body, but it is well with my soul." The suffering of the outward man often results in the maturing of the inward man. *"Though our outward man perish, yet the inward man is renewed day by day."* (II Corinthians 4:16)

Yes, suffering does accomplish valuable good in us. It conditions us to greater usefulness in this life, and it also secures great reward for us in the world to come. *"For I reckon that the sufferings of this present time are not worthy to be compared with the glory which shall be revealed in us."* (Romans 8:18) We need to try to see this by faith. Paul understood this when he wrote, *"I Paul am made a minister; who now rejoice in my sufferings."* (Colossians 1:23,24) Peter also exhorts us, *"But rejoice, inasmuch as you are partakers of Christ's sufferings; that, when his glory shall be revealed, you may be glad also with exceeding joy."* (I Peter 4:13)

When Christ suffered, such a joy was set before him that enabled him to endure the cross. There is a similar sustaining joy for all of us who suffer, which we must set our eyes upon. Health and Wealth doctrine overlooks this and deprives many well-deserving saints of the comforts of God, for their suffering is not in vain, as much as their labor is not in vain.

Health and Wealth doctrine overlooks this and deprives many well-deserving saints of the comforts of God, for their suffering is not in vain, as much as their labor is not in vain.

We can be so narrow minded and short sighted. We are so far from comprehending the intricate, profound workings of God. Such a purging and inner building takes place in us in times of pain, only the surface of which we usually see. *"Where were you when I laid the foundations of the earth? Will you also disannul my judgment? Will you condemn me that you may be righteous?"* (Job 38:4; 40:8) Science has hardly begun to understand the super complexities of the human psyche and body. How much less do we grasp the mind of God and His dealings with us. If our understanding of His ways have progressed six feet, then we have as far to go as the nearest stars to understand Him just a little. (See Isaiah 55:10)

"And his disciples asked him, saying, Master, who did sin, this man, or his parents, that he was born blind? Jesus answered, Neither has this man sinned, nor his parents: but that the works of God should be manifest in him."

(John 9: 2,3)

10

What About Christians Who Get Sick or Suffer?

If a Christian gets sick, is that a sign God is punishing them? Does it mean God is angry with them? If they're sick, does that mean they just don't have enough faith? If a child of God is going through a period of suffering or loss, is that an indication of God's displeasure with them? Stay with us, folks; the Bible once again gives us clear answers, and it is good news.

We must not fall into the rut of accounting everyone who is ill or suffering some health setback as being punished by God. Not every sickness or tragedy is a judgment of God. Maybe not even the majority. Neither is good necessarily an indication that God approves of a man's ways. "Healthy" does not equal "holy" any more than "rich" equals "right".

The "health and wealth" crowd are, no doubt, very well meaning and have the best of intentions for us all. They would love to see us all financially secure and in good health. This sentiment, the apostle John shares, *"Beloved, I wish above all things that you may prosper and be in health, even as your soul prospers."* (III John 2) However, the reality is, we all fall short of this pleasant ideal. And there shall always be those who fall short, *"You have the poor with you always."* (Mark 14:7) It is just as likely that we shall never find the cures for every known sickness, so that we could say, "The sick we shall have with us always." It seems pretty clear that sickness, death, sorrow, crying and pain shall be with us until these former things are passed away and God shall wipe away all tears from our eyes. (Revelation 21:4) This is partly because of the fallen nature of man and partly because if we were always healthy and wealthy, we would not be so wise. Allow me to explain. There are two important principles to be understood on the subject of Christian suffering. First -

I. Suffering May Accomplish Good Through Us.

One much overlooked fact is that commonly, a great deal of good happens to people who get sick, or hurt, or incur some disability. Joni Erickson Tada has been a sterling example. Our Lord knows how not only to deliver his righteous ones out of all their afflictions, but also how to actually work good out of them. Thus, He makes us more than conquerors. By our afflictions, he works good *in* us and *through* us.

Possibly the most moving, insightful hymn writer of modern times is Fanny Crosby, blind nearly all her life. Such a grace of God was upon her! So humble was she that most of the thousands of pieces she wrote were submitted under pseudonyms. It seems that because she was not so distracted by the things of this world, she acquired an insight and discernment of spiritual things rarely found in others.

> *"Blessed assurance, Jesus is mine!*
> *Oh, what a foretaste of glory divine!*
> *Heir of salvation, purchase of God,*
> *Born of his Spirit, washed in His blood...*
>
> *Perfect submission, perfect delight,*
> *Visions of rapture now burst on my sight:*
> *Angels descending bring from above*
> *Echoes of mercy, whispers of love..."*

She seems to see *"visions of rapture"* and hear *"echoes of mercy"* most of us do not. She seems to have such a *"foretaste of glory divine"* that most of us do not. I'm not saying that blind people automatically get such spiritual aptitudes. Rather, first she apparently gave her life to Christ: *"Jesus is mine"*, and then also gave him *"perfect submission"*. Once she did though, it appears that God showed more to her than to the usual believer. But it was *"to profit withal"*, to benefit the church at large. I am sorry that Fanny Crosby was blind, but highly grateful for the good God worked through her.

In 1873, Horatio Spafford and his family planned to visit Europe. Due to business obligations in Chicago, his wife and four daughters traveled ahead of him. In November, the family embarked on *S. S. Ville du Havre*. While en route, the ship was struck and sank so suddenly that all four daughters died, while Mrs. Spafford survived. She cabled her husband the heart-breaking news, "Saved alone". Soon after, Mr. Spafford sailed to meet his wife in England. While at sea, the ship captain sent word to Spafford that they were at the approximate location where the *Ville du Havre* went down. Spafford went up to the weather deck of the ship by night to view that parcel of the sea that was the tomb of his perished children. At such a poignant, melancholy time, the inspiration of God came upon him. As the waves rolled off the bow of the ship, these words were formed in his mind:

> *"When peace, like a river, attends my way,*
> *When sorrows like sea billows roll;*
> *Whatever my lot, Thou hast taught me to say,*
> *It is well, it is well with my soul...*
>
> *My sin – oh the bliss of this glorious thought:*
> *My sin not in part, but the whole*
> *Is nailed to the cross and I bear it no more,*
> *Praise the Lord, praise the Lord, O my soul!"*

No one knows how many untold millions have been ministered to by the penetrating words of this hymn. Sometimes it seems that only those who have hurt deeply can connect with those who hurt deeply. "*Deep calls unto deep*". (Psalm 42:7) In some mystical way, deep suffering or anguish works in us a depth of compassion, insight and connection with others in like state. There is a refining, perfecting that occurs in us when we suffer, whether it's a migraine headache, an uncomfortable pregnancy, persecution, diabetes or bereavement. *How* the suffering occurs doesn't seem to be as important as *that* the suffering occurs.

This is the principle taught in I Peter 4:1,2: "*Forasmuch then as Christ has suffered for us in the flesh, arm yourselves likewise with the same mind: for he that has suffered in the flesh has ceased from sin; That he should no longer live the rest of his time in the flesh to the lusts of men, but to the will of God.*" Now this does not teach us to be masochists or ascetics, intentionally bringing suffering upon ourselves. This seems rather to encourage us in the suffering we already get, that there is purpose and benefit in it. The passage sets Christ as our example. We know that he did not at all invite or seek suffering for himself. "*O, my Father, if this cup may not pass away from me, except I drink it, thy will be done.*"

Neither did he shy away from it. Jesus' suffering was God ordained and prescribed. Likewise for us. Jesus' suffering provides us inestimable benefit in the redemption of our souls. Our own suffering similarly works in us incalculable benefit in the sanctification of our souls; that is, our perfecting, nurturing, and being conformed to the image of Christ.

Notice the powerful, priceless benefit of suffering, "*he that has suffered in the flesh has ceased from sin.*" In our case, suffering does not entirely deliver us from sin, but it sure puts it nicely in remission. To the extent that we suffer, sin is defeated in us. This is similar to parents curing their children of sin by spankings, etc. "*Whom the Lord loves he chastens, and scourges every son whom he receives.*" (Hebrews 12:6)

However, not all suffering is chastening or punishment. Remember the disciples asked Jesus, *"Master, who did sin, this man, or his parents, that he was born blind? Jesus answered, Neither...but that the works of God should be manifest in him."* (John 9:2,3) This is not to say that the parents and son had never sinned, but that the blindness was not a result of their sins. In others, some suffering is intended to display the glory of God in man; in others, suffering displays the providence of God in man.

II. Suffering Can Display the Providence of God.

In the spring of 1977, I was stationed in Bremerton, Washington, a new believer attending a small Baptist church. It had been the desire of our pastor for some time to start a bus ministry. At about that time, twenty or so of my friends and I got together every Saturday afternoon for several hours of tackle football. It was a very enjoyable highlight of the week for us. One fateful afternoon, I was tackled from behind and sprained my ankle bad enough to be out for the season.

The following Sunday in church, I took to heart our pastor's interest in the bus ministry for the first time. Previously, my good health was actually a hindrance to serving God. Well, a few of us "conspired" to give our pastor his wish. We waited until he was out of town for two weeks and raised the $4000.00 needed to buy a full-sized school bus and surprised him with it when he returned. Soon the time came to go out visiting the community to recruit riders for our new bus. Since I was no longer able to play football on Saturdays, I volunteered to help. As you might expect from folks in the military, we planned our strategy very carefully. After much prayer one Saturday morning, two teams of us set out about 1 P.M. We gave out fliers to every house and were careful to follow the chain of command in approaching the parents first in inviting the children to church on our bus. The folks we met were very polite, but after three hours, we had absolutely zero success. The other teams stopped and went home, but my teenage partner and I persisted. As we approached the door of one house, a strange thing happened. A single word seemed to be whispered into my mind. It occurred to me that God was saying, "Stop." I stopped halfway up the driveway, puzzled. My partner looked at me, questioningly. Then a second word came to my mind as if someone had said to me, "Listen." That was all. No explanation. Naturally, I listened to the sounds around me, still standing halfway up somebody's driveway. One sound in particular caught my attention: the sound of children playing in the distance. No further word or message or guidance. Just "stop" and "listen". I wondered, "Is this the Lord speaking to me? Does the Lord want me to go to where I hear those children playing? Wait a minute, Lord. We can't do it that way. We can't talk to the children first; that's not following the chain of command." Then it seemed again like God was talking to me, "How well is your way working?"

At that, I said to my partner, "come on, we're going to try something different. We meandered through the neighborhood following our ears. We discovered that the source of sound was a small neighborhood playground where about a dozen children were playing. We finally found some children, except now we had no plan. I stood there completely at a loss how to proceed. Then I figured that whatever I was going to say, I may as well say it all at once. I yelled out, "All you kids come here a minute!" Amazingly, every one immediately stopped and walked straight over to me, solemn-faced. They probably wondered if they were in trouble. Actually, I was the one in trouble. I still had no idea what to say. I almost said, "Never mind," and walked off. Instead, I blurted out, "Whoever rides our bus to church tomorrow, we'll take them to Baskin and Robbins after and buy them all the ice cream they can eat." I instantly regretted saying that. I was ashamed of stooping to such tactics as bribery to get kids to church. Why didn't I think more before I spoke? Well the children had an entirely different reaction. They erupted into a loud raucous cheer! "Revival" broke out. Everybody wanted to go to church. Chattering like little birds, they all asked excitedly, "Can I come? Can I come?" We explained that we'd have to ask all their parents. Then eleven year old Ian insisted, "Me first!" He took my hand and began pulling me in the direction of his house. I was numb with disbelief. The entire crowd of children, ranging from five years old to twelve years old, followed us to Ian's house. On the way, I remember thinking, "Well, now comes the hard part." Was I in for a surprise. We all came to Ian's house and he knocked on the door. A little puzzled, I asked him, "Don't you live here?" He replied, "Yes." I asked him, "You have to knock to go in your own house?" He said, "Oh, yeah." and grinned. Then he went inside and brought his mother to the door. When I introduced myself and explained my business, Ian's mother smiled and said, "That's a good idea. I've been wanting Ian to go to church." Dumbstruck, I said, "You have?" She said, "Sure. What time does he need to be ready?" After we made arrangements, we proceeded to the next child's house. I thought to myself, "Well at least we found one kid to go to church tomorrow. I wonder if we'll find another?" The identical thing happened at the second home, except that the child didn't knock on his own door. Again the parents were glad to sign up their kids for the church bus. I was totally mystified. After two hours and about a hundred attempts, we had zero success. Now using an approach that didn't even make sense, we were two out of two.

On the way to the third house, I noticed that three girls on bicycles had joined us. As we continued making the rounds, we picked up more and more children. I felt like the pied piper. It was phenomenal to me that after about four stops, not one parent turned down our request. Then something dawned on me: as each parent came to their door and was presented with the request to allow their child to go to church, they were looking at the familiar faces of all the neighborhood children. They were probably assuming that all those children were also going to our church. So they must have thought, "Well, if all these kids are going, my child may as well go, too." Even Ian's mother, at the first house must have assumed the same thing, except that so far, no one was going. However, by the third or fourth house, some of the kids *were* going. So, catching on, I pointed out to the parent, "Ian, here, and Dana and Julie are coming. Could your children come, too?" Now add that to the insistent pleas of their own children and the parent didn't stand a chance.

The outcome was that we went on "harvesting" till nightfall. The next morning, as the church bus picked up twelve children for our first Sunday, a certain joy became imbedded in my heart that has never faded. After a month, attendance was up to thirty one, including a couple of teenagers and parents. In that first month, nine children came to Christ and were baptized. Sadly, I had to leave at that point and return to San Diego, my home port.

One little ten year old girl named Julie was very notable to me. She and her friend, Dana, had pleaded to be brought to church on Sunday nights as well. So each week, I brought them. All the children were encouraged to invite their parents and evidently Julie was very dutiful about this. I believe it was my last Sunday morning in town that Julie boarded the bus, her eyes filled with tears. She sat by me and covered her face. I put my arm around her and asked, "Julie, what's wrong?" Julie's father had become tired of her asking him to come to church and he gruffly told her that if she ever asked him again, she would not be allowed to go back to church herself. I felt sorry for her, but I was speechless.

We parted ways that Sunday afternoon with promises to write and see each other again someday.

About four months later, I took a week of leave to travel to Bremerton to visit them again. What joy I had riding the church bus again, seeing all "my" bus kids and now quite a few more. To this day, it remains one of the happiest occasions of my life. A little sorrow touched my heart when, amid all the happy chattering, I noticed the bus drove past Julie's house without stopping. Julie must have asked Daddy one too many times, I thought. Still we absolutely reveled at our reunion.

When we arrived at church, I got off the bus nearly last. Just as I stepped to the ground, some little person met me with a bear hug and a squeal of delight. But I couldn't tell who it was seeing only the top of their head. When I knelt to the ground to get a better look – it was Julie! Excitedly, she took my hand and said, "Come see a surprise!" A few steps away stood a grinning Dad, Mom and older sister, dressed for church, Bibles in hand. A couple of months before, the whole family had turned to Christ, got baptized and hadn't missed church since.

What does all this have to do with a chapter on suffering? Simply that these victories for Jesus all resulted from a sprained ankle. Christian fruitfulness so often stems out of Christian suffering. The providence of God allowed my injury, which in turn resulted in a wondrous string of events.

Christian fruitfulness so often stems out of Christian suffering.

What about Christians who suffer? We can be sure it is only by God's permission. When sinners suffer, it is either a judgment of God or God drawing someone to Himself. Either way, God intends good for him. When Christians suffer, it is either a chastening work of God, or a refining work of God, again, intended only for the Christian's good.

"When through fiery trials thy pathway shall lie,
My grace all sufficient shall be thy supply;
The flames shall not hurt thee, I only design
Thy dross to consume and thy gold to refine."

Though we are seldom aware of the benefit during the process, we can be sure that our heavenly Father sees to it *"that all things work together for good to them that love God."* (Romans 8:28) Whether we get promoted or laid off, God works it out for our good. Whether our child makes honor roll or is bedridden, God works it out for our good – and theirs. This verse seems to address the seeming setbacks of life, more than the apparent advancements, because the good intentions of God are easy to see in the blessings of life. So Romans 8:28 is a reassurance to us that even when things look bad, God is still very much working on our behalf. God was just as surely working good in Joseph in prison as when he was elevated to the throne of Egypt. God is just as surely working good in us when we get cancer as when we are in perfect health. The one who is in great health is not necessarily more in favor with God than the one who contracts Parkinson's disease or hepatitis.

III. Is Continued Health Trouble a Sign of Weak Faith?

Not at all. Even though misleading statements would tend to make us think so. "Well I don't read where Jesus ever turned down someone wanting to be healed." However, Paul asked three times that God would remove his *"thorn in the flesh"*, and God turned him down. Yet God did so in order to increase the grace and power on Paul's life.

"Well if you had enough faith, God would heal you." But if *this* person had enough faith, he could pray for the sick one and they'd recover. I've always wanted to get the phone number and address of the people who say this so I can ask them when they get sick, "What's the matter? Don't *you* have enough faith?" (Don't you hate it when you think of these great comebacks about a week too late?) The truth is: if we had enough faith and discernment to see what God is working in us through that very condition, we would not ask for healing nearly so often.

Is continued health trouble a sign of weak faith? If we base our answer on evidence around us, we'd have to say: continued health trouble is more a sign of *developing* faith. Paul's enduring his *"thorn in the flesh"* resulted in the power of Christ resting upon him. We must *"let patience have her perfect work."* When God declines our request for restored health, it is surely in order to give something better. We should still pray effectually and fervently for healing in every case anyway, because we don't know when God is ready to heal. But let us ask in faith, nothing wavering.

Is continued health trouble a sign of weak faith? We've asked and asked to be healed, but to no avail. Is it because we have not had enough faith when we asked? I believe it is more likely a sign that God has great confidence in His choice child, as with Job. God does not so much *inflict* suffering upon us, as *entrust* us with it.

God does not so much inflict suffering upon us, as entrust us with it.

When the High Majesty said, *"Whom shall I send, and who will go for us?"* (Isaiah 6:8), he was asking, "Who can I entrust with this message? Whom can I trust with the associated suffering? Who can suffer the shame, bear the awful burden and eventually be killed for my name's sake", as Isaiah did? Every priceless saint of God who endures the cross of suffering ordained for them is highly honored by God. May God grant them the grace to endure patiently, without complaining, to keep faith in Him unwaveringly, never doubting His love for them or His good plans for them. This must not be just to put on a good appearance before men; but because God wants to show off his child before the courts of heaven.

IV. What! Me Suffer?

With all this talk about the benefits of suffering and hardships, the implication is that we're all supposed to get some, that we all could benefit from afflicting circumstances. But wait! What if I don't want it? What if I'm not interested? Well, God doesn't need our permission or ask our advice. Of course, we're always giving him advice anyway. But God is sovereign and he decides and prescribes for each of us, while we are unqualified to do so. Parents understand this. Whoever heard of a kid who said, "Dad could I get a flu shot?"

There are some who avoid suffering and such negative experiences. They like to consider themselves exempt from grief, crippling conditions or chronic pain since they have worked so hard for the Lord. Maybe they would excuse themselves from the hardships of missionary service because they already give financially to such work.

In answer to this, consider how Moses dealt with the tribes of Gad, Reuben and the half tribe of Manasseh. Israel's armies had already conquered the land bordering the Jordan River on the east side. These three tribes had a lot of cattle and noticed that the east side of Jordan was an excellent place for cattle to graze. (Lot noticed the same thing and it got him in trouble.) It seemed reasonable, then, when they asked Moses if they could settle in that land. It was a very comfortable land, a land of plenty, a place of ease since the cities and houses were already built. It was the easy course. The only problem was: the other nine and one half tribes had yet to conquer the land of Canaan, where they were to settle. So when presented with the rather selfish request, Moses replied, *"Shall your brethren go to war, and shall you sit here?"* (Numbers 32:6) The question for American Christians, likewise living in a land of plenty and ease might be:

- Shall Jesus suffer the cross, and shall we sit here?

- Shall Stephen and Paul be stoned, and shall we sit here?
- Shall the martyrs be burned at the stake and shall we live in our ease?
- Shall the thousands of current missionaries endure hardships as good soldiers of Jesus Christ and shall we sit here, relaxed, complacent, enjoying?
- Shall missionary David Brainerd suffer an early death by tuberculosis and shall we sit here? Brainerd sacrificed his health by living in severe conditions among the Indian tribes of New England.

We seem to have the idea that modern American Christians are the only ones exempt from suffering. Too much does Peter still say, "*Master, spare thyself.*"

V. An Amazing Story.

In 1921, David and Svea Flood left their homeland of Sweden and moved to a very primitive region of the Belgian Congo (now Zaire) with their two year old son. With another couple (the Ericksons), the Floods began the long arduous trip deep into the dense jungles. They were attacked by suffocating heat and by every insect imaginable. The two families struggled for many days through the dense jungle underbrush and through frequent attacks of malaria. In extreme fatigue, they finally stopped near the village of N'dolera. They were soundly refused any contact by the native people. Their agonizing struggle for survival against the elements and against sickness wore on them for several months.

On top of their physical sufferings, they also ached with the sense of dismal failure to win Africans to Christ. With all contact with the tribe at N'dolera cut off, their efforts and suffering seemed to be in vain.

Only one young boy was allowed to visit the missionaries to sell eggs and chickens. While the others tried fruitlessly to make inroads with the villagers, Svea Flood focused on the little boy, befriending him and showing him love. She was able to win him to Christ. But no successful contact was ever made with the village people.

Their suffering with malaria, depression, malnutrition and fatigue stretched out to many months. The discouragement was so severe that the Ericksons finally left. The Floods might have left with them, except that Svea was pregnant and weak with malaria. An attempt to make the rugged trip back would be life threatening for her. As it was, when Svea gave birth to the child, she struggled to survive, in and out of consciousness, finally losing the battle with malaria after seventeen days. In utter anguish, David buried his beautiful twenty-seven year old wife in a grave he dug with his own hands. Despair set in. David was unable to continue living in this land that was nothing but torment to him. He decided to quit and return to Sweden.

Before he left the Belgian Congo, he gave his new baby, a girl they named Aina, to the Ericksons. Soon after, both Ericksons also died. How could such suffering be allowed to these gracious, well-intentioned, persevering Christians? How could their lives be thus expended for nought or, seemingly, for so little? My God, my God, have you forsaken them? The baby, Aina, then came under the care of a third missionary couple, the Bergs, who moved back to the United States about two years later.

Meanwhile, David Flood grew bitter against God. He later re-married, but never attended church again. His life developed into a series of tragedies, compounded by a severe drinking problem. Things went steadily downhill for him for many years. Unlike Job, who kept his integrity and had his fortunes restored and his family replaced; and unlike the just man who *"falls seven times, and rises up again"*, David

Flood did not rise up again and did not have his fortunes restored. Was all that suffering in vain? Was Svea's death in vain? Did the Ericksons die in vain?

Forty years passed. Little Aina was renamed Aggie and grew up in a fine Christian home, later attending North Central Bible College in Minneapolis, Minnesota. There she met and later married Dewey Hurst in 1944. Years later, Dewey became president of Northwest College in Kirkland, Washington. While there, strange things began to happen.

For years, Aggie Hurst had quietly longed to visit Sweden in hopes of finding her real father. One day, her dream came true. At their twenty-fifth anniversary, The Hursts were given a surprise by the college: round trip tickets to Stockholm, Sweden. This was a shock to Aggie because she had never told anyone at the college of her desire to visit Sweden. The very day their flight was scheduled to leave, a magazine arrived in her mailbox anonymously. It was a Swedish magazine, but she couldn't read a word of it. Inside was a picture of a grave with a white cross inscribed with the name "Svea Flood". Realizing it was her mother's name, she made a mad dash to the home of Doris Olson, a Swedish teacher at the college.

The article told the story of two missionaries traveling through the Belgian Congo who found the white cross pictured just outside the village of N'dolera. One missionary told the other the story of Svea Flood, how she had died shortly after giving birth to a baby girl. The story continued, giving details Aggie had never heard. She read (or rather, had it read to her) that Svea had won the little boy to Christ. Later that boy grew up to build a school in his village. He led each of his students to believing in Christ. The students went home and won their parents to Christ. Eventually, the village chief also came to Christ. The article ended by reporting that there were over 600 Christians living in N'dolera as a result of Svea's faithfulness and the sacrifice of several missionaries.

Remember, Aggie Hurst discovered all this the day she and Dewey left for a visit to Sweden. Upon arrival in Sweden, Aggie met her long lost brother, her three step brothers and her step sister. Though the family was very disjointed, troubled and estranged from their father, Aggie persuaded them to visit him together. Knowing what a religious person Aggie was, the family strictly warned her not to mention God to David Flood or he would go into a rage.

He was seventy-three now, suffering from diabetes, debilitated with a stroke, nearly blind and virtually bedridden for three years. When they met, they embraced with tears, but when Aggie mentioned that God had taken care of her, David recoiled angrily and blamed God for all his troubles. Then Aggie spoke these words to her father, "Papa…you didn't go to Africa in vain. Mama didn't die in vain. The little boy you won to the Lord grew up to win that whole village to Jesus Christ. The one little seed you planted just kept growing and growing. Today, there are 600 African people serving the Lord, because you were faithful to the call of God in your life." Right there, in tears, David Flood ended more than forty years of bitterness and resentment against God. He prayed and asked God's forgiveness. A few weeks later, he died. But they had not heard half the story.

Sometime later, Dewey and Aggie traveled to London for a conference. Practically on a whim, they attended a preaching meeting at Royal Albert Hall. At one point, Christian leaders from around the world were introduced. One black man was introduced as the leader from Zaire. He presented his report, "In Zaire, we have thirty-two mission stations, many large schools, a one hundred and twenty bed hospital and have 110,000 baptized believers…" Aggie was stunned. After the meeting she found her way to the man, Ruhigita Ndagora. Imagine her shock when she discovered that this man was that little boy her mother had won to Christ over forty years ago! When Ndagora discovered that

Aggie Hurst was Svea Flood's little baby, which he had seen, he wept and said, "I've so often wondered whatever happened to that little white girl whose mother died for us. Thank you for letting your mother die so that we can live." Svea Flood and her baby girl had become a legend in Zaire.[7]

What about Christians who get sick or suffer? Their sufferings are sometimes the instrument of God birthing something great, as a woman's labor pains result in a new life. For a child of God, it may be a new ministry, a spiritual awakening, widespread salvation or the converting of entire households. Generally, it seems that the benefit of the suffering far exceeds the extent of suffering. The result is that many will glorify God concluding, *"this is the Lord's doing and it is marvelous in our eyes."* It is not necessary that the suffering saint be directly connected to the wonder that God shall bring to pass. However, we could reasonably expect that it would happen nearby and that the sufferer would be aware of it. In the case of Adoniram Judson, he was the direct instrument of a phenomenal work of God. In the case of Svea Flood, the great work that resulted from her suffering was linked to her, but occurred posthumously.

What about Christians who get sick or suffer? It is a privilege and honor. We become partakers with Christ in sufferings. As his death resulted in the eternal salvation of all who would believe in him, so the subsequent suffering or death of many to come would follow the pattern of Jesus Christ, in working benefit for those around them. How many saints may someday echo the words, *"I...now rejoice in my sufferings for you, and fill up that which is behind of the afflictions of Christ in my flesh for his body's sake, which is the church."* (Colossians 1:24) They may not have meant it so, but God makes it so.

"See now that I, even I, am he, and there is no god with me: I kill, and I make alive; I wound, and I heal: neither is there any that can deliver out of my hand."

Deuteronomy 32:39

Does God Show Preference as to Whom He Heals?

As we discussed in chapter 9, some are healed and some are not. All things being equal (seemingly), some folks are blessed with a supernatural healing or restoration, while in other cases, no such thing happens, even though Godly men and women prayed sincerely. Why this is will probably always be somewhat of a mystery. Our God is a mysterious God; He is an awesome God; His ways are past finding out. We will never be able to completely figure Him out. He still cloaks Himself in darkness, and His ways in obscurity, yet He is pleased to reveal somewhat of His ways and his wisdom to us. He still reveals His secrets to his servants the prophets. *"It is the glory of God to conceal a thing: but the honor of kings is to search out a matter."* (Proverbs 25:2) Let's take this verse as an invitation to explore the issue of why some folks are healed and others are not. Who knows? Maybe God will reveal this unto babes.

I. Principles Learned From the Eight People Raised From the Dead.

A study of the many healing type miracles done in the Bible shows an interesting trend. Some of the miracles of the Bible give no indication of the character of the person receiving the healing. However, there are many cases where the beneficiary is a righteous person. On the other hand, there are virtually no recorded cases of healing done for a wicked person. Of course, we know that our Lord is gracious every day to the sinner and saint alike. Every day, He gives provision of light, joy and love even to the least deserving of us. But indications are that He largely reserves His special dispensations of providence for a select, favored group – not entirely, but largely. We cannot put God in a box, or state with certainty what He will or will not do.

Let's pick one group of miracles in the Bible to analyze and see what we may learn from them. One manageable group would be the eight recorded incidents of dead bodies being raised to life. To summarize those incidents:

a. (I Kings 17) Elijah raises back to life the son of the widow of Zarephath.
b. (II Kings 4) Elisha raises back to life the small son of the Shunamite couple who housed him.
c. (II Kings 13) Shortly after Elisha died, another man was being buried. During the burial, enemy Moabites came suddenly. The men performing the burial hastily deposited the body in the nearby sepulcher of Elisha. When the dead body touched the bones of Elisha, *"he revived, and stood up on his feet."* (II Kings 13:21)
d. (Matthew 9) Jesus raises back to life the twelve year old daughter of Jairus, the ruler of the synagogue.
e. (Luke 7) Jesus raises to life a man being carried to his grave, who was the only son of a widow in the city of Nain.
f. (John 11) Jesus raises back to life Lazarus, who had been dead and in the grave four days.

g. (Acts 9) Peter raises up the deceased widow, Dorcas.
h. (Acts 20) Paul raises back to life Eutychus, a man who fell to his death from the third floor of a building where Paul had been preaching.

These are eight of some of the most marvelous demonstrations of the power of God through the instrumentation of man. Much may be said about when these great, divine works were done, since in every case, a key man of God and his message were vindicated by the miracle. In all of these eight instances, we hear loud and clear the message, *"I am the resurrection and the life."* The God whom we serve has power not only to raise up to life dead bodies, but also to put spiritual life into formerly dead souls. Both of these mighty, divine works shall culminate simultaneously at the resurrection of the just, when we shall be perfected, glorified and transformed into children of God. These eight instances of resurrection along with our personal experiences of spiritual rebirth are assurances to us that what God has promised, He is able to perform in the great day. What blessed assurance we have of heavenly things to come!

The God whom we serve has power not only to raise up To life dead bodies, but also to put spiritual life into formerly dead souls.

These eight resurrections span old and new testaments and were accomplished by not only Jesus himself, but by apostles and prophets. The resurrection is for saints of the gospel era as well as for saints of the old covenant. We also see that divine power is administered frequently in partnership with man in performing miracles. This applies to times before Christ, to Christ's time and to the days following Christ and the apostles.

Let's take a look now at the individuals who were raised back to life. What kind of people were they? Were such mighty graces of God extended to a random group of people or were they applied to those on whom the favor of God rested?

In the first instance, what kind of woman was the widow of Zarephath? (She was the one who truly received the benefit of the miracle, since the boy was her son.) First we note that she was a widow. She had already suffered much sorrow in losing her husband. She was also a victim of the great famine which had struck the land. She and her son had suffered much hunger, thirst and deprivation. In spite of all these hardships, she was very kind to Elijah when he approached her and asked her for food. All she had left was one handful of meal, yet she gave Elijah a portion first. God rewarded her by miraculously supplying her with food for the duration of the famine. She was also caring enough of her relatives to share the food supply with them, as Rahab saved the lives of all her kin whom she brought into her house at the fall of Jericho. The woman also provided room and board for Elijah during the same period of time. It is not clear whether she knew it or not, but she was harboring a fugitive from the king, which could have gotten her in big trouble. Because of the fame of Elijah, I think she probably did realize what she was doing. Later when her son became sick, she had the faith to request Elijah's help, and the humility to confess her sins. She also expressed her faith by saying, *"I know that you are a man of God, and the word of the Lord in your mouth is truth."* (I Kings 17:24) This was about as worthy a woman as one could find. It was because of her faith and righteousness that Elijah went to none of the many widows in Israel, but rather to this foreigner. (Luke 4:25,26) In this case, the miracle of raising someone to life was done for a very worthy person.

The second instance is similar to the first. In the first case, it was for a poor woman. In this case, it was for a well to do woman of the city of

Shunem. She apparently saw Elisha visiting town and noticed that he was homeless and probably without food. She extended an invitation to him to eat at her house. It seems at first that he declined and that she became a little more insistent, for the Bible says, "*She constrained him.*" (II Kings 4:8) She is of the same class as righteous Lot, who also saw strangers in his city and he "*pressed upon them greatly*" to eat at his house. When they consented to come, "*he made them a feast.*" What a pleasant contrast such righteous folk make with the perverted generation around them. In the case of the Shunamite woman, she extended her hospitality to Elisha (and Gehazi, his assistant) every time he came to town. Later, she and her husband built an apartment onto their house and fully furnished it solely for the use of Elisha. Again, the miracle of raising a dead child back to life was done for a very righteous woman.

In case number three, in which the dead body was hastily placed on the bones of Elisha in his sepulcher, and the body "*revived, and stood up on his feet*", we're told nothing about what kind of people were involved in this shocking, but very happy incident. We know nothing about the man who had been deceased or about the men who had been preparing to bury him.

So the score is now:

Righteous folk raised:	2
Not known:	1
Sinners raised:	0

In case four, the man getting the benefit of the miracle was a very religious man, the equivalent of a pastor, for he was "*one of the rulers of the synagogue.*" (Mark 5:22) He had enough faith in Jesus to travel some distance to bring his request to him. He was a reverent man and he bowed down at Jesus' feet and worshipped him. His faith was such that he was not shy about asking Jesus to heal his daughter even though she was at the point of death. Once again, we find the miracle being done for a righteous man.

Case five is found in Luke seven. This is the second case where the son being raised back to life is the only son of a widow. Here, though, we're told nothing about what kind of people the mother and the son were. So we have another "Not known."

Case six is found in John eleven and is probably the most famous. This is when Jesus raised up Lazarus after being in the grave four days. Lazarus was the brother of Martha and Mary, who were all very good friends of Jesus. They lived in a town called Bethany, which was close to Jerusalem. It was this Mary who had anointed Jesus with ointment and wiped his feet with her hair. How she loved and worshipped him! It was such a love they shared with Jesus that when word was sent to inform Jesus that Lazarus was very ill, the note was worded, "*he whom you love is sick.*" Scripture also plainly states, "*Now Jesus loved Martha, and her sister, and Lazarus.*" (John 11:5) This family loved Jesus and often served dinner to him and the apostles. This family later suffered persecution for their loyalty to Jesus. So we have yet another clear case of a resurrection miracle being done for a righteous man, or family, in this case.

The seventh incident is the story of Dorcas, a saintly woman who died suddenly. Dorcas was "*full of good works and almsdeeds which she did.*" (Acts 9:36) Later, at her wake, the Bible says, "*all the widows stood by him (Peter) weeping, and showing the coats and garments which Dorcas made.*" Dorcas actively did good for people all around her, especially for folks who needed it most such as these widows. "*Pure religion and undefiled before God and the Father is this, to visit the fatherless and widows in their affliction.*" (James 1:27) Without question, Dorcas was very much a righteous woman. She is a model of a virtuous woman for ladies of all generations. "*She seeks wool, and flax, and works willingly with her hands...*

she lays her hand to the spindle, and her hands hold the distaff*...she stretches out her hand to the poor; yes, she reaches forth her hands to the needy."* (Proverbs 31:13,19,20) When all of Dorcas' widow friends approached Peter with stories of her kindness to them, it is not clear whether they presented this as a basis for Peter attempting to raise her from the dead. What we do know is that these reports are in the scriptural record for a reason. All scripture is *"profitable."* Peter dismisses all the weeping crowd and kneels beside the body of Dorcas alone. Maybe the fresh reports of her goodness in Peter's mind fueled his prayer with some earnest and fervor. What we do know is that Peter prayed and Dorcas arose from the dead. Score one more for the righteous.

The final incident of someone being raised from the dead is found in Acts 20. Paul was preaching on his last day in the city of Troas. This was also about the last time Paul preached publicly in the region where he had planted so many churches. It is likely that everyone realized that Paul would never return to Troas, so Paul preached through the night to give the Christians there the maximum benefit of his time. Faithful men and women gathered together to hear the word of the Lord. These Godly folk had such a hunger and thirst for righteousness that they tarried all night taking in the excellence of Paul's preaching.

These folks are said to be *"disciples"* and Eutychus was one of them. At about midnight, Eutychus, who had already been hearing Paul's preaching for hours, dozed off to sleep and fell from a third floor loft. The fall was fatal, and he died immediately. Paul rushed down to where the body was and embraced it. The life of the man returned to him and when all the people saw it, they were *"not a little comforted."* (Maybe we better stay awake in church.) This was a very timely miracle because it powerfully vindicated the message and ministry of the apostle Paul. Clearly, Eutychus was a righteous man.

---

* Parts of a spinning wheel.

The final score is now:

Righteous folk raised:	6
Not known:	2
Sinners:	0

So of the eight incidents of dead folk being raised back to life, at least six (maybe all) of them were notably good people, or it was done *for* a notably good person, as the Shunamite woman. God seems to do miraculous wonders like these largely for righteous and, if we may say, deserving folk. It cannot be confirmed that one of these eight folk was a sinful person. Even though we know that God is kind to the unthankful and to the evil.

How do we apply all this? We should pray for the recovery of the righteous and unrighteous alike. We should lay hands on and pray for the healing of someone living in sin as well as for a saintly person. We should pray for the healing and restoration of folks near us at every opportunity regardless of their lifestyle. As David said, *"Who can tell whether God will be gracious?"* Or to whom He will be gracious. Maybe the goodness of God healing an unlikely sinner will lead him to repentance out of gratitude. On the other hand, if we have opportunity to pray for the healing of a Godly soul like Dorcas, we may have stronger faith and higher expectations that God will act for this one.

II. A Tale of Two Kings

Let's make an interesting comparison between two kings of Israel. You probably know about King Hezekiah and the terminal illness he contracted. The prophet Isaiah visited him while he was sick and said, *"Set your house in order; for you shall die."* (II Kings 20:1) Hezekiah's response was, *"he turned his face to the wall, and prayed unto the Lord, saying, I beseech you, O Lord, remember now how I have walked before you in truth and with a perfect heart, and have done that which is good in your sight. And Hezekiah wept sore."* Hezekiah was hardly boasting; he was greatly understating the good he had done. Scripture highly commends his character, work and leadership. He was arguably the best king of all those that came after David. Notice that all Hezekiah's prayer consisted of was a modest mention of his faithfulness to the Lord. Hezekiah had faith enough to ask of God even though it looked pretty bad. Let's face it, when Isaiah the prophet, speaking by the word of the Lord, says you're going to die, things aren't looking good. Yet he asks anyway and God heals him and grants him fifteen more years. I have the feeling that Hezekiah's goodness was at least part of the basis for God healing him. Maybe his righteousness was recompensed in the earth.

The second king is found in II Kings 1:2, *"And (King) Ahaziah fell down through a lattice in his upper chamber that was in Samaria, and was sick: and he sent messengers, and said unto them, Go, enquire of Baalzebub the god of Ekron whether I shall recover of this disease."* His majesty, King Ahaziah, was not a good man. Scriptural records tell us *"He did evil in the sight of the Lord."* (I Kings 22:52) This may strike you as strange, that a king of Israel would turn to a false god and not ask of his own God, but Ahaziah was an idolater. He sent messengers to enquire of Baalzebub, a god of the Philistines, even though this king had a capable prophet and healer close to him by the name of Elijah. The two knew each other and Elijah was acquainted with his father, the former King Ahab. Elijah intercepted the messengers and sent word back to the king, *"Is it not because there is no God in Israel, that you go to enquire of Baalzebub, the god of Ekron?"* (II Kings 1:3) Today, the rebuke would be, "Is there no God for you to turn to that you would go to fortune-tellers and professional advisors for your answers? Is there no God to answer when you call upon Him?" Elijah also delivered this word of the Lord to Ahaziah, *"Now therefore thus says the Lord, you shall not come down from that bed on which you are gone up, but shall surely die."* A short time later, Ahaziah did die, having reigned only two years.

Why didn't Ahaziah get healed like Hezekiah did? Besides the fact that he did not ask from God, he was a wicked man. If he had been a good man who simply didn't know to ask God, God might have sent someone to point him in the right direction, as Peter was sent to Cornelius. It seems probable that Ahaziah's wickedness had something to do with not getting healed. *"Though a sinner do evil a hundred times, and his days be prolonged, yet surely I know that it shall be well with them that fear God...but it shall not be well with the wicked."* (Ecclesiastes 8:12,13) It is a frequent judgment that wicked men do not live out half their days. (Psalm 55:23)

If we expect God to heal us some day, we better behave now. At least our odds will improve. The righteous seem to fare better than others in receiving miraculous cures. Pestilence and destruction shall come upon the wicked, but regarding the righteous, God's word says, *"a thousand shall fall at thy side, and ten thousand at your right hand; but it shall not come near you."* (Psalm 91:7) General Sennacherib, with his 185,000 plus soldiers, threatened and insulted King Hezekiah and the God of Israel, boasting how no god could stop them from sacking the besieged Jerusalem. Yet tens of thousands of Assyrian soldiers died suddenly overnight, while Hezekiah and his men were untouched. The remnant of the once mighty Assyrian army limped home in humiliated defeat.

God is good and gracious to everyone, but righteous, honest, good people seem to get more of God's special, miraculous assistance than others.

God is good and gracious to everyone, but righteous, honest, good people seem to get more of God's special, miraculous assistance than others. When Jesus healed the cripple at the pool of Bethesda, we find evidence that he was a God-honoring, grateful man, for *"afterward, Jesus finds him in the temple."* (John 5:14) It is interesting to note that Jesus healed *only* this man although there were with him *"a great multitude of impotent folk, of blind, halt, withered."* (John 5:3) Why did he choose to heal this man over all the others? We can only guess, but the Bible makes it very clear that he was a worthy, good man. I can't help but think he was the most deserving. God may invite Rahab and the demoniac into the family of faith, but His select gifts, callings and providences, He dispenses to the likes of Nathaniel, an Israelite in whom was no guile, and to Zecharias and Elisabeth, who were both *"righteous before God and …blameless."* (Luke 1:6)

When Peter and John healed the cripple in Acts 3, we again find a man who was righteous and grateful. First of all, he chose to seek his welfare at the temple of God, rather than at the gates of the city, where there would have been a lot more traffic. Then once he is cured, he gives liberal praise to God as he happily enters the temple with the apostles. What little is said of this former cripple shows a very good heart; and Peter perceived that God was choosing to heal this good man.

Does God have preferences as to whom He heals? The jury is still out, but the evidence leans heavily toward a conclusive "yes."

“Beloved, believe not every spirit, but try the spirits whether they are of God: because many false prophets are gone out into the world.”

I John 4:1

12

Try the Spirits

How do we test the spirits to see whether they are of God or not? How do we tell if a preacher is properly or falsely representing God? First, we see if their words align with God's word. This is not as easy as it might seem. False prophets and even Satan himself quote scripture well enough, but then misapply it. *"And he brought him to Jerusalem, and set him on a pinnacle of the temple, and said unto him, If you be the Son of God, cast yourself down from here; for it is written, He shall give his angels charge over you, to keep you; And in their hands they shall bear you up, lest at any time you dash your foot against a stone. And Jesus, answering, said unto him, It is said, You shall not put the Lord, your God to the test."* Typically, false messages tend to flatter and encourage worldliness and self-serving. For example, preachers of false messages sound churchy and religious enough, making liberal use of Bible passages. The most dangerous and effective ones look good, sound good and make you feel good. The best counterfeits look most like the true ones. So it is essential that we know not only the words of the Bible, but the sense and intent.

For example, someone might easily misapply what Jesus said to the adulterous woman, *"Neither do I condemn you"* by concluding that we are not to condemn people living together immorally. Yet we know from numerous other verses that it is a fundamental responsibility of Christians to speak out against sin, to reason with sinners so that they would turn from their wrong-doing for the safety of their souls. Not doing so would be to do them the greatest possible disservice. If we neglect to warn the wicked against their ways, they will die in their sins, but God will hold us guilty for not warning them.

If we are going to earnestly contend for the faith, we better be well-versed in its truths. There is no short cut to this. We must read, study and meditate on the Bible, not just once completely through, but as a life style – every day. We cannot take "False Doctrine 101" and become experts in error detection. We must become as familiar with the teachings, principles and characters of the Bible as we are with our own families. We should know Boaz and Balaam as well as our own brothers; we should be as familiar with Martha and Michal as if they were our sisters. We should come to be as knowledgeable of God, his works and his ways as to be able to say, "That sounds like something God would say." A husband hears a friend tell some incident involving his wife and he says, "that sounds just like her" because he knows her so well. He can also tell when a story about his wife is untrue. How does a couple get to know each other so well? By spending a lot of close time together.

I. How to Spot a False Prophet.

If it looks like a skunk, smells like a skunk, walks like a skunk and sounds like a skunk, it probably is one. There are traits of a false prophet which may help us identify them and be on our guard against them.

1. A false prophet will speak what is popular, whether it is right or not. Paramount in their mind is winning the approval and applause of man. No message could be more popular than the idea that God wants me to have the best and wants me to be in

perfect health. Such a message (and consequently the messenger) will be eagerly received, right or wrong.

2. A false prophet will *not* speak what is unpopular, even if it is the right thing to do. He would not endanger his popularity or his appeal to others by preaching against sin, drinking, immorality, homosexuality, avarice or gambling. Such preaching would not be in his interest as this might alienate some of his followers. Jesus was a true prophet, willing to preach the good news and the bad news. He preached the whole counsel of God, not some sugar coated, watered down message. He was willing to preach against sin. *"Woe unto you, scribes and Pharisees, hypocrites! You serpents, you generation of vipers, how can you escape the damnation of hell?"* Not particularly tactful, but it was precisely what his hearers needed at that time. John the Baptist, Peter, John, Paul and other apostles preached hard-hitting messages like that as well. *"O full of all subtlety, and all mischief, you child of the devil, you enemy of all righteousness, will you not cease to pervert the right ways of the Lord?"* False prophets don't preach like that. They're more into sweet talking us. How about these winsome words of Peter: *"Your money perish with you…for I perceive that you are in the gall of bitterness, and in the bond of iniquity."* We *sure* won't hear that out of false prophets today. They would prefer that all men would speak well of them, yet Jesus warned, *"Woe unto you, when all men shall speak well of you! For so did their fathers to the false prophets."* (Luke 6:26)
3. A false prophet is not set on pleasing God or serving His kingdom, but serves his own agenda. That agenda may be to rise within the denominational ranks, to build his own "kingdom", church or ministry, or to gain power or wealth. If the tendency

of a man's words is to attract a following to himself or to increase the wealth he has control over, it smells like a skunk. He will say he serves God; he will seem to serve God, but in reality he serves himself. This may be very apparent or it may be well cloaked. But eventually, the tree will be known by the fruit it bears.

4. False prophets are quick to declare that they are right and that everybody else is wrong. They defend their position forcefully and charismatically, but cannot do so scripturally. We must not be so naïve as to believe everyone we hear. We ought to search the scriptures daily to see if their words are true.
5. False prophets are notorious for taking scripture verses out of context. They will apply the verse in a way it was never intended. They ignore numerous other passages that speak clearly to the contrary. For example, Psalm 84:11 is taken to mean God will give us anything we desire if we live right. "*No good thing will He withhold from them that walk uprightly.*" But this in no way justifies us in having material excesses. God would not tell us in one verse that we may have anything in this world our heart desires and then in other verses say things quite the contrary. "*Love not the world, neither the things that are in the world.*" "*But woe unto you that are rich! For you have received your consolation.*" "*Is it a time to receive money, and to receive garments, and oliveyards, and vineyards, and sheep, and oxen and menservants, and maidservants?*" (II Kings 5:26)

The problem lies in who defines "*good things*" and "*walks uprightly.*" If *we* draw the line between righteous and unrighteous, we'll draw ourselves into the "righteous" side every time. "*All the ways of a man are clean in his own eyes.*" Similarly, if we define "good things", we will include everything *we* find desirable, whether it's good for us or not. So it's important to know –

II. What are the *"good things"* of Psalm 84:11?

First, let's take a look at the rest of the verse, where we will see false prophets have clearly taken part of the verse out of context. The whole verse reads, *"For the Lord God is a sun and shield: the Lord will give grace and glory: no good thing will he withhold from them that walk uprightly."* This verse (and the entire psalm) is highly exalting the gracious goodness of God. It particularly focuses on the most magnificent gifts of God toward man. He enlightens the heart of his believers as the sun brightens the day; he is a shield and a defense to them that love him; he bestows his own grace (spiritual gifts and character) to them that ask; he gives glory, eternal glory, to those who honor him; all such good and perfect gifts will he give to those children adopted by faith. That's what the verse is saying. Consider what a misfit it would be to interpret the third phrase in a worldly sense. "For the Lord God is the brightness of sunshine to our soul; he is shield, defense and protection to us: he bestows his very grace, spirit and character into our hearts: and he gives us money and nice houses." Say what? It just doesn't fit. Now God is kind and does indeed allow us to have good jobs and nice homes. But these are not the good things God has in mind to give us. Anyone who interprets this verse to mean God would give us any material or worldly thing we desire has a very worldly viewpoint to begin with. So what are the *"good things"* God would not withhold from them who walk uprightly? Let's hear from Jesus on this.

38. *"Now it came to pass, as they went, that he entered a certain village; and a certain woman, named Martha, received him into her house.*
39. *And she had a sister, called Mary, who also sat at Jesus' feet, and heard his word.*

40. *But Martha was cumbered about much serving, and came to him, and said, Lord, do you not care that my sister has left me to serve alone? Bid her, therefore, that she help me.* 41. *And Jesus answered, and said unto her, Martha, Martha, you are careful and troubled about many things.*
42. *But one thing is needful, and Mary has chosen that good part, which shall not be taken away from her."* (Luke 10: 38 -42)

Jesus commends Mary for choosing "*that good part*" or "good thing", which in this case would be the rich preaching of the word of God. What makes it a "good thing"? The fact that it is good *for* us. Good for the soul. Good influence on us.

We find help from another Mary in defining "*good thing*". In Mary's prayer of Luke 1, she expounds, "*He has filled the hungry with good things; and the rich he has sent away empty.*" (v. 53) What are these "*good things*"? Whatever it is, the rich don't have it. They are sent away empty. In worldly things, they are "*rich and increased with goods*" (and in their opinion) "*have need of nothing*", but in actuality, they have nothing of the real "*good things*"; they "*know not that (they) are wretched, miserable, poor, blind and naked.*" The "*good things*" Mary mentions, which are given to those who hunger and thirst for it, would be the righteousness of God, the blessed gospel, spiritual endowments of gifts, the indwelling Holy Spirit, free access to the Father, divine visions, golden truths, wisdom and the love of God shed abroad into our hearts. What price can be put on such good things? This is the spiritual birthright of the children of God. Then in the world to come, it shall be our Father's good pleasure to give us the kingdom. Let's not be as Esau, who despised his birthright, preferring more immediate gratification. "*Feed me, I pray thee…what profit shall this birthright do to me?*" But the rich are not sent away empty *because* they are rich, but because they did not hunger for God's "good things". They chose the wrong "good things" to set their hearts on. This was the error of the rich man.

"There was a certain rich man, who was clothed in purple and fine linen, and fared sumptuously every day." (Luke 16:19) Here is a man who had done well for himself, as folks would say. We may assume he was a very nice man, always dressed well. He had a fine upscale home and all the good things money could buy. He fared sumptuously. I can just hear him say, "God sure has blessed me. I am clearly experiencing divine favor. He has given me the desires of my heart." He lived life to the fullest. The problem was, he kept it all for himself; he had no heart for the poor. We're not told that the man was a heavy drinker or lived with his girlfriend or sinned in some other way. We may assume he was a pretty good fellow by man's standards. We even find evidence that he was a church-going man. This man lives in every city and suburb in the United States. And he died and went to hell. From hell he pleaded his case. The reply from heaven was, *"Son, remember that you in your lifetime received your good things, and likewise Lazarus evil things; but now he is comforted, and you are tormented."* (Luke 16:25) Likewise, when future Babylon falls, the reason is given, *"How much she hath glorified herself, and lived deliciously, so much torment and sorrow give her."* (Revelation 18:7) Jesus has forewarned, *"Woe to you who are rich, for you have received your consolation."* (Luke 6:24) Notice the reason heaven gives for the rich man, or rather, the formerly rich man, being in hell, *"you...received your good things."* That is, he preferred earthly "good things" over heavenly "good things". Matthew Henry points out that it is not said that he *abused* riches, but that he *received* them. If he had asked, God would gladly have given him a new heart and fruit of the Spirit, such as love, joy and goodness. Then he could have been like Zaccheus and cheerfully provided Lazarus some nice meals and maybe a place to stay. God was ready to show him the way of eternal life, but he was too preoccupied with the pleasures of this

life. The rich man grew up amid a wealth of the word of God, as all the Jews did (and as all Americans do), yet he was willingly ignorant of it. As much as his brothers did, the rich man had Moses and the prophets. We will all be held accountable for the instruction, wisdom and Godly counsel we *could* have had.

Where else are *"good things"* mentioned? Consider Matthew 7:11. *"If you then, being evil, know how to give good gifts unto your children, how much more shall your Father, who is in heaven, give good things to them that ask him?"* Taking this in the context of the surrounding verses, Jesus is assuring us that, as a good Father, God will give us only what is good for us, never anything otherwise. In Luke 11:13, he clarifies what he means by *"good things"*, *"If you then, being evil, know how to give good unto your children, how much more shall your heavenly Father give the Holy Spirit to them that ask him?"* Above all else, "good things" means the Holy Spirit. Oh sure, God lets us get good things of this world for ourselves, but the best of this world compared to God's "good things" are like chaff compared to gold. But if we choose our "good things" over God's "good things", he would be just in withholding his.

In Romans 10:15, we read, *"And how shall they preach, except they be sent? As it is written, How beautiful are the feet of them that preach the gospel of peace, and bring glad tidings of good things!"* The parallelism in this verse makes *"good things"* and *"gospel of peace"* equivalent expressions. And what would those good things be? The wondrously good news that peace has been established between God and man; that the door of eternal life has been opened by the presenting of an acceptable sacrifice. "Good things" would be the fact that a man's sins may now be atoned for and paid off once and for all, and that he may be made acceptable to God the Father through having Jesus. God help us to value such good things now in this life as much as we will in eternity!

Can you see now, that in the Bible, "good things" means heavenly treasure, not earthly? *"Every good gift and every perfect gift is from above, and comes down from the Father of lights, with whom is no variableness, neither shadow of turning."* (James 1:17)

III. Does God Give Us the Desires of our Heart?

"Delight yourself also in the Lord, and he shall give you the desires of your heart." (Psalm 37:4) As with Psalm 84:11, many try to use this verse as a blank check to get whatever they want in this life. Is this what God meant? As a matter of fact, it is. However, the verse says that the granting of the desires of the heart applies only to those whose desire and delight is God. We cannot use this verse to "claim" a job promotion or a late model car. If we have our heart set on those things, we are not delighting ourselves in the Lord. Therefore, we are disqualified from using the verse. But if the desire of our heart is to know him and to love him more and more, then he will grant such a desire of our heart. This is like, *"Blessed are they who do hunger and thirst after righteousness; for they shall be filled."* Does this mean that God would not bless someone in giving them a new, reliable car or a nice raise? Not at all. He probably does so every day. God is more gracious than we can imagine. He patiently bears with our immaturity and misplaced affections. He realizes that we are a work in progress. But God may or may not choose to give us the worldly desires of our heart. Granted, sometimes he does, out of his benevolence. But for those who desire God himself and his good things, this verse guarantees them the fulfillment of their wish.

IV. Conclusion.

Is it God's will that we have health and wealth? It certainly is, but by his definition, in his time, and in his way. No one has higher goals for us than our heavenly Father. No one wants the absolute best for us more than he does. No father holding his newborn infant in his arms ever held more cherished ambitions and higher aspirations for his child's future than our heavenly Father does for us. He is going to work out his plans for us, with or without our approval, our knowledge, or even our cooperation. Isn't that how our parents raised us?

God decides what good things we will get, even though our selfishness or stubbornness may stall the process. We are assured in scripture that, "*he which has begun a good work in you will perform it until the day of Jesus Christ.*" (Philippians 1:6) We want good physical health; God wants us to have good spiritual health – as well as good physical health. We want comfort and ease; God wants us to have character and virtue. Now he's fine with us having the comfort and ease, too, as long as we're not lacking in Godly qualities. If we are lacking, he's perfectly willing on our behalf to forfeit the lesser to obtain the greater. So heartaches, hurts and handicaps sometimes come to those, for a season, in whom God is doing a work. As soon as his purpose is achieved, he restores our comforts, as with Job. Typically, we do not enjoy the process, any more than a child enjoys homework; but we later savor the excellent results, as when that child graduates with honors. We may not like the way God drives, but we'll be very happy with the destination he brings us to.

We want to live the "good life" and surround ourselves with the best that money can buy. Yet God wants us to have inner wealth such as wisdom, spiritual perception and compassion. Of course, he loves to see us happy with pleasant accommodations in this life. But that is secondary in God's economy and should be in ours, too.

Sometimes, too much material wealth hampers our growth in spiritual wealth. When I was in the Navy, a few of my buddies and I regularly visited an orphanage we found in one of the seaports we frequented. We developed close friendships with the well-mannered children we met there. After three months, our ship was due to leave. As a going away present for our little pals, we bought them a couple of little tricycles, a couple of small bikes and a wagon. They had never had such nice toys and they were extremely happy to get them. But a very disturbing thing happened. There were five toys and about forty kids. They soon began fighting over the toys, each one wanting their turn to ride. The children, who had been so close knit and loving toward each other, now fussed and fought with each other. So the material good we gave them resulted in the detriment of their character. (This also happens among adults.) I felt terrible about the development, but didn't know what to do. I'm sure glad I don't have God's job. God, in his wisdom, sometimes withholds or removes those things that are a detriment to our maturing.

For some of us, we agree well enough with God's plans for us, but we aren't happy with the timing. We want all our prosperity and good things *now*. We want our success and achievement *now*. Never mind the several rounds of failure or sickness that condition us for success. For those of us who are impatient, God's process can be agonizingly slow. May he give us glimpse enough of the excellence of his ways to give us perfect peace with his timing.

Lastly, and luckily, God is going to do things his way, in spite of all the advice we give him. (Just like husbands.) We might prefer to go through a season of hard work to refine our character; God may decide that a bout with cancer will better accomplish his will in us. Or God may choose painful financial setbacks to purify our values. Some of us would scream in protest, "No, Anything but my money!", thus validating God's choice.

God is going to do good for his born again children; he is going to do it in his way; and he is going to do so whether we like it or not. He is willing to risk our resentment of him for a while to work out excellent good for us in the meantime. Such patient, longsuffering love does he have for us!

"I am come that they might have life, and that they might have it more abundantly." (John 10:10) This verse summarizes God's benevolent will for us. Yes, he'd be pleased to see us healthy and wealthy; but these fall subsidiary to his higher aims and ambitions for us. We want to live like kings and queens, but God wants to *make* us kings and queens.

It is my prayer that this book will enlighten your understanding of God's will for your life and give you a beacon of hope to encourage you in the dark times. May God richly prosper you.

THE END

Bibliography

1. *King James Bible*

(Chapter. 2)

2. CEO WORLD Magazine, August 24 issue, "With a GDP of 26.85 trillion USD, the United States is by far the world's largest economy in this ranking for 2023".
3. Information Plus, *Compact, Gambling: Who Wins?* 1998 ed., 2812 Exchange St. Wylie, Texas 75098

(Chapter. 5)

4. *C. T. Studd, Cricketer & Pioneer,* Norman Grubb, CLC Publications, Fort Washington, Pennsylvania 19034

(Chapter 6)

5. *Matthew Henry Commentary,* Fleming H. Revell Company, Old Tappan, New Jersey. Vol. VI, p. 269.

(chap. 10)

6. *One Witness,* Aggie Hurst with Doug Brendel, published by Chosen Books, Fleming H. Revel Co., Old Tappan, New Jersey

About the Author

I am a 69 year old born again Christian who has been active in a variety of churches for 47 years. Observing Christians in America during that time has given me cause to worry about our collective spiritual state. One disturbing trend is the lack of knowledge of Bible truth. I am concerned that we as a people will perish for lack of that knowledge. It seems that only a small minority of church-going Americans have read the Bible through even once. This makes us vulnerable to every wind of doctrine that blows across our land. I am not an expert on the Bible and certainly not an expert sociologist. But I do enjoy trying to present the Bible in a clear and enjoyable way. It has always been enjoyable to me. Bible preaching and teaching has been a part of my life for over 30 years.

I am the second of ten children. Our father, Ray Stieffel, Jr., was also an author. I have admired his writing since I was a child and have always wanted to be a writer like him. This desire finally connected with my spiritual concerns and resulted in Health and Wealth: God's Will or Not?

I live in Bay St. Louis, Mississippi and enjoy the water and sailing. Currently attending First Baptist Church in Bay St. Louis.

About the Author

Printed in the United States
by Baker & Taylor Publisher Services